Wide range of delicious
vegetarian and non-vegetarian

Dishes and Desserts

from four corners of India

Tanushree Podder

Publishers
Pustak Mahal®
J-3/16 , Daryaganj, New Delhi-110002
☎ 23276539, 23272783, 23272784 • *Fax:* 011-23260518
E-mail: info@pustakmahal.com • *Website:* www.pustakmahal.com

Sales Centre

- 10-B, Netaji Subhash Marg, Daryaganj, New Delhi-110002
  ☎ 23268292, 23268293, 23279900 • *Fax:* 011-23280567
  E-mail: rapidexdelhi@indiatimes.com
- **Hind Pustak Bhawan**
  6686, Khari Baoli, Delhi-110006
  ☎ 23944314, 23911979

Branches

Bengaluru: ☎ 080-22234025 • *Telefax:* 080-22240209
E-mail: pustak@airtelmail.in • pustak@sancharnet.in
Mumbai: ☎ 022-22010941, 022-22053387
E-mail: rapidex@bom5.vsnl.net.in
Patna: ☎ 0612-3294193 • *Telefax:* 0612-2302719
E-mail: rapidexptn@rediffmail.com
Hyderabad: *Telefax:* 040-24737290
E-mail: pustakmahalhyd@yahoo.co.in

ISBN 978-81-223-0626-2

Edition: June 2011

Printed at : Unique Color Carton, New Delhi

Dedication

I dedicate this book to
my grandmother
and my mother,
both of whom were
superlative cooks.

Acknowledgements

This book would not have been possible without the support and encouragement of my loved ones. I would like to thank Anupriya for all the work she has put in bringing out this book. Without her suggestions and contributions, I couldn't have written this book. We spent long hours discussing the recipes that should go into the book.

I would like to thank my husband for the role he played as the guinea pig on whom I have been trying out all my culinary experiments through the years. He patiently bore all the suffering without ever discouraging me.

A big thank-you goes to all the friends, relatives and neighbours who shared their precious recipes with me.

Preface

As a young girl, I was a tomboy who loved climbing trees and playing rough games. As a result, I hardly learnt any cooking. It was when I got married to a defence officer and had to host many parties that I realised my handicap. It was then that I seriously began learning the intricacies of cooking.

That was the time when I collected recipes by the dozen, pestering each and every cook for the instructions, and tried out different recipes. Sometimes they were a success but most of the time they were a disaster. I wrote many humorous pieces on my cooking and bore the brunt of my friends' jokes. But I was made of a stern stuff. Relentlessly, I pursued my goal. Success can't elude people who persevere and it didn't let me down, either.

Having learnt the hard way, I was determined that I should translate all my recipes into a book so that others could benefit from it. Writing a book on cookery can be a very humbling experience. When one begins to translate the experience into words, it somehow becomes a formidable task. It is difficult to put all that one knows into a written form.

Cooking is an art, one that requires a lot of patience and perseverance. As I travelled all over the country, I began picking up recipes and learnt the intricacies of dishing out local flavours. I realised that there was a treasure of cuisine culture in our country. In a melting pot where all types of languages, customs and practices co-existed, there were different types of food which defied all definitions.

A Bengali by birth, I am truly cosmopolitan in my upbringing. I remember my mother trying out various types of dishes, from all regions, when I was a girl. She had collated many recipes from relatives, friends and neighbours. When I grew up, I inherited her notebooks with all the recipes. In the course of years, I continued to add recipes to those notebooks and the volume grew.

Experience plays a very important role in cooking. With experience one instinctively knows how much of a particular spice to add to a particular dish. Most experienced cooks, I met, did not measure the spices with teaspoons but doled out portions with their hands. I was told that they depended on their judgement to measure out the ingredients. When I began experimenting with my judgement, I faced many difficulties. It took a long time before I could succeed in putting some of the recipes together.

It is amazing how the food habits differ from place to place. There is a lot of difference in the cooking that is done in the southern part of Kerala and the northern part of Kerala. Similarly, East Bengal has a different set of rules from West Bengal. A person from one end of Tamil Nadu cooks the *sambar* in a different manner than another person from Karnataka. The same curry will find different flavours in different parts of Andhra. The culinary practices also differ in different castes from the same region. Brahmins cook the *sambar* in a different manner while the other castes will cook the same dish differently.

The ingredients differ from state to state. Most ingredients are based on the local availability. The dishes made in the coastal area use a lot of coconut because it is easily available. The flavours differ from region to region. While the Bengali cooking requires mustard oil, the dishes cooked in Kerala require coconut oil. It is the tamarind which is used in the South while Goans use kokum and vinegar. Just a little variation in a single ingredient can make a substantial difference to the dish.

As one keeps experimenting and trying out new dishes, one discovers the amazing range of delicacies one can churn out, with just a few modifications. What is required is just a little imagination and a whole lot of creativity.

When I started the book, I did not know where to begin. A few hundred pages are not enough to put together the plethora of recipes that are available in each region. After much deliberation, I selected the popular and the easy ones from each region to include in this book. I have tried to stick to traditional recipes since I feel that there is no tastier food than the ethnic and traditional ones. To this day, grandmother's cooking happens to be far tastier than the new fangled recipes.

None of the recipes given in this book have been invented by me. They have been around for decades. I am just a tool who has had the opportunity to compile and collate them and present them in this book.

One important thing that I would like to bring out is that anyone and everyone can be a good cook. All it takes is a little effort and lots of creativity. If I could do it, so can you!

—Tanushree Podder

Contents

Chapter-1

The Northern Platter

From the green valley and gurgling streams of Kashmir to the land of Nawabs at Lucknow, through the vast expanses of the mustard fields in Punjab, the Northern belt has a surfeit of recipes that can take one's breath away. Mention the word Kashmir and one is inundated with images of the tall chinars, beautiful belles and *shikaras* on the Dal Lake. The *Wazwan* remains a test of culinary skills for the ultimate chef from the valley. The staple diet of Kashmiris remains the rice and meat dishes and one who has tasted *gustaba or kahwa,* can never forget the experience. Famous for the red chillies, fruits, nuts, saffron and *rajma,* Kashmiri cuisine is a rich blend of these ingredients.

From Kashmir to Punjab, the journey may not be a very long one but the cuisine is quite different. For the earthy people of Punjab, eating is a pleasure to be pursued with equal vigour and energy exhibited in their local *bhangra.* The *sarson da saag* and *makke di roti* is an unforgettable combination for any Indian. Washed down with a glassful of *lassi,* it can be a hearty meal by itself. The variety of vegetables and meat dishes found in Punjab can fill many books. Whether it is the *chana masala* or the fish fry, the process of cooking is very different from that of other regions. A lot of stress is placed on the onion-garlic-ginger combination along with a liberal use of tomatoes.

From the land of the Nawabs come the *Mughlai* dishes that have become a gourmand's delight all over the world. The rich flavour of these culinary delights can make the tongues drool with excitement. The succulent *kababs* and the tongue tickling taste of flavoured *parathas* have sent many a poet into raptures. *Mughlai* cooking is the legacy of Mughals who were fond of good food. The blending of spices over low heat and extracting the inherent flavour of each ingredient is important in *Mughlai* cuisine.

Saag-Sabjiyan

Whenever the words Mughlai *cooking or* Kashmiri *cuisine are mentioned, visions of non-vegetarian food flood our minds. Although it is true that most of the non-vegetarian dishes from the North of the country are famous for their distinctive taste; there are several vegetarian items which are equally famous. The unbeatable* rajma, chana *and* bhartas *are deliciously ruling the roost in most restaurants and hotels. Whether it is the* Navratan Korma *or the* Paneer Pasanda, *the vegetarian food from the North has a place of its own in the world of culinary delights. Think of stuffed* bhindis, *brinjal* bharta *and cauliflower preparations and you will realise the contribution this specific region has made to the field of vegetarian delicacies.*

MASALA BAINGAN *(Spicy brinjals)*

Ingredients

- ½ kg small round brinjals
- 300 gms tomatoes, chopped
- 1 onion, chopped
- 150 gms freshly grated coconut
- 3 tbsp sesame seeds
- 1 tbsp ginger-garlic paste
- 1 tbsp chilli powder
- 3 tbsp coriander powder
- 2 tbsp garam masala powder
- ½ tbsp turmeric powder
- ½ tbsp poppy seeds
- 3 cloves
- 3 bay leaves
- 2 cardamoms
- A few coriander leaves
- A few mint leaves
- 7 tbsp oil
- Salt to taste

Method

- Roast the sesame seeds and poppy seeds on the tawa till brown. Pound them into a fine powder.
- Heat oil and fry the onions till brown.
- Grind the sesame-poppy powder, tomatoes and freshly grated coconut to a fine paste.
- Cut brinjals into long and thin slices.

- Heat oil and fry the brinjal slices till they become soft. Remove from oil and keep aside.
- Add cloves, cardamoms and bay leaves to the remaining oil. Also add coriander leaves and mint leaves for flavour.
- Add ginger-garlic paste and coriander powder. Fry lightly for a minute.
- Add the masala paste and fry well for about 3 minutes.
- Add chilli powder, salt, turmeric powder and garam masala powder. Fry till the oil floats on the top.
- Add fried brinjals and cook on low heat for a few minutes with a lid on.
- Garnish with coriander leaves and serve hot with chapatis.

KHOYA MAKHANA

(Puffed lotus seeds with khoya)

Ingredients

- 100 gms khoya
- 50 gms makhana (puffed lotus seeds)
- 100 gms peas, shelled
- 15 cashewnuts
- 3 tomatoes, chopped
- 2 green chillies
- 1 tbsp cumin seeds
- 2 tbsp coriander powder
- ¼ tbsp turmeric powder
- 1 tbsp garam masala
- 1 tbsp dry ginger powder
- ½ tbsp amchoor powder
- 3 tbsp ghee
- 1 tbsp sugar
- Salt to taste
- Oil for frying

Method

- Roast the khoya on a tawa till light brown.
- Add the sugar to 1 cup of water and boil the peas in it till soft.
- Deep fry the cashewnuts and makhana separately and keep aside.
- Heat the ghee in a pan. Add cumin seeds, ginger powder, green chillies, turmeric powder, coriander powder, amchoor powder, garam masala and salt.

- ❖ Add the khoya, sliced tomatoes, boiled peas and cook for 5 minutes.
- ❖ Lower the flame, add ½ cup water, fried makhana and cashewnuts. Simmer for 5 minutes and remove from the fire.
- ❖ Serve hot with parathas or naan.

CHATPATE CHANE *(Spicy chanas)*

Ingredients

- 600 gms chana
- 2 onions, sliced
- 2 tomatoes, chopped
- ½ tbsp red chilli powder
- ½ tbsp amchoor
- ½ tbsp cumin seeds
- ½ tbsp ground anardana
- ½ tbsp kasuri methi
- 50 gms ginger juliennes
- 4 bay leaves
- ¼ tbsp sodium bicarbonate
- 100 gms ghee
- ½ tbsp coriander powder
- 2-3 cinnamon sticks
- ½ tsp pepper powder
- 1 tbsp garam masala
- 100 gms tamarind
- 1½ cup water
- ½ tbsp roasted cumin seeds
- A few coriander leaves
- 2 green chillies
- Salt to taste

Method

- ❖ Clean and wash the chana and soak it overnight. Add sodium bicarbonate to it.
- ❖ Boil the chana in the same water along with a teaspoon of salt.
- ❖ Heat ghee in a pan and fry the sliced onions till golden brown.
- ❖ Add finely chopped tomatoes, red chilli powder, amchoor powder, cumin seeds, anardana, kasuri methi, ginger juliennes, bay leaves, and fry well.
- ❖ Add cinnamon sticks, garam masala and coriander powder, roasted cumin powder, stir well.
- ❖ Add the water and cook for a while till a thick masala gravy is obtained.

- Soak tamarind in 1½ cup water and extract a thick pulp. Sieve the pulp and mix in the red chilli powder, salt and pepper powder in it.
- Add the thick masala gravy to the boiled chana, mix the tomato pulp and cook for 5 minutes.
- Garnish with finely chopped green chillies, coriander leaves, onion rings and serve hot.

DUM ALOO SHALIMAR

(Baby potatoes in thick gravy)

Ingredients

- 550 gms baby potatoes, boiled
- 125 ml curd
- 1 green chilli, deseeded and chopped fine
- 2 tbsp ghee
- 10 gms coriander leaves chopped fine
- 1 tbsp fennel seeds
- ¼ tbsp garam masala powder
- Salt to taste

For Masala Mix

- ½ tbsp cumin powder
- 1 tbsp coriander powder
- ¼ tbsp black pepper powder
- ½ tbsp turmeric powder
- ½ tbsp ginger powder

Method

- Peel the potatoes and prick them all over with a toothpick. Melt the ghee over medium heat in a pan and fry the potatoes till the outer layer turns brown, turning them over frequently. Remove and set aside.
- Remove the pan from the fire and add the fennel seeds followed by the masala mix. Lower the heat and place the pan back on the flame, fry for a minute.
- Add curd and salt and mix well.
- Add the fried potatoes. Cover the pan and simmer for 10-12 minutes.
- Add garam masala powder and remove the pan from heat.

- Stir in the coriander leaves and the chopped green chillies.
- Serve hot with chapatis.

SHAHENSHAHI ALOO
(A delicious potato preparation)

Ingredients

- ½ kg potatoes
- 1 small tomato
- 1 large onion
- 2 cups curd
- 8-10 mint leaves
- 2 green chillies
- Few coriander leaves
- 1 tsp poppy seeds
- ½ tbsp garam masala
- 2 black cardamoms
- ½ tbsp red chilli powder
- ½ tbsp cumin powder
- ½ tbsp coriander powder
- 1 tbsp butter
- Oil for frying
- Salt to taste

Method

- Peel and prick potatoes with a fork.
- Grind together onion, poppy seeds, mint, chilli powder, cumin powder, coriander leaves, green chillies and cardamoms.
- Boil potatoes with a little vinegar so that they retain their whiteness. Add 1 teaspoon butter to the potatoes.
- Heat oil, fry the ground masala for 5-7 minutes. Add curd and tomatoes. Fry for 3 minutes.
- Put the potatoes and fry for another 5 minutes.
- Add garam masala and salt. Add 1 cup water and cook on low heat.
- Garnish with coriander leaves and serve hot with chapatis.

NOORJEHAN KOFTA CURRY

(Cottage cheese balls in spicy curry)

Ingredients

- 300 gms crumbled paneer
- 100 gms potatoes, boiled and mashed
- 50 gms bread crumbs
- ½ tbsp garam masala powder
- 1 tbsp poppy seeds
- ½ tbsp cumin seeds
- Salt to taste
- 3 tbsp oil for gravy
- Oil for deep frying

Grind to Paste

- 300 gms tomatoes
- 1 pod garlic
- 1" piece of ginger
- 2 tsp chilli powder
- ½ tbsp turmeric powder

For Garnishing

- 100 gms grated coconut
- 2 tbsp coriander leaves

Method

- ❖ Mix paneer and mashed potatoes, divide the mixture and shape into small balls.
- ❖ Roll in bread crumbs and deep fry in hot oil. Remove and keep aside.
- ❖ Heat 3 tbsp oil and season with cumin seeds and poppy seeds.
- ❖ Add tomato-ginger-garlic paste and fry till the oil floats on top. Add the rest of the masalas and fry for 5 minutes.
- ❖ Add a little water and make a thick gravy. Add the fried koftas, salt and simmer for about 10 minutes.
- ❖ Sprinkle garam masala powder. Garnish with coriander leaves and grated coconut. Serve hot.

NAVRATAN KORMA

(Cottage cheese with mixed vegetables. Navratan means: nine gems. As the name suggests, it was initially created to give the flavour of nine vegetables)

Ingredients

- 150 gms paneer, diced and fried
- 3 cups of mixed vegetables: potatoes, green peas, beans, carrots, cucumber, cauliflower (boiled)
- 4 tomatoes, chopped
- 3 onions, chopped
- 1 tbsp ginger-garlic paste
- 1½ cup milk
- 4 tbsp fresh cream
- 4 tbsp ghee
- ½ tbsp turmeric powder
- 2 tbsp coriander powder
- 3 tbsp chilli powder
- 1½ tbsp garam masala powder
- Salt to taste

Method

- Heat oil and fry onions.
- Add the ginger-garlic paste and fry for 2 minutes.
- Add tomatoes, turmeric powder, coriander powder, chilli powder, garam masala and salt. Fry for 5 minutes.
- Add all the vegetables, milk, cream and fried paneer. Cook for a few minutes till the vegetables and paneer are done.
- Serve hot.

PINDI CHANA

(A famous chana preparation from Punjab)

Ingredients

- 400 gms kabuli chana
- 20 gms gram flour
- 5 tbsp oil
- ½ tbsp ajwain
- 3 tbsp anardana powder
- 2 tbsp amchoor powder
- 1 tbsp chilli powder
- 1 tbsp black salt powder
- ½ tbsp kasuri methi powder
- 1 tbsp cumin powder
- Salt to taste
- 1 pinch of soda bicarb

For The Pouch

- 6 black cardamoms
- 2" stick of cinnamon (powdered)
- 4 cloves
- 20 gms ginger (crushed)
- 1 tbsp tea leaves

For The Garnishing

- 2 tomatoes (sliced)
- 1 onion, cut into roundels and separated into rings
- 2 green chillies, slit and deseeded
- 3 lemons, cut into wedges
- 10 gms ginger, julienned, and soaked in 2 tbsp lemon juice

Method

- ❖ Soak the kabuli chana overnight.
- ❖ Tie the ingredients for the pouch in a small piece of muslin cloth.
- ❖ Boil the kabuli chana with soda bicarb and 1 litre water.
- ❖ Add 4 tbsp oil and pouch, cover and simmer until cooked (the chana should not get mashed).
- ❖ Heat the remaining oil, add the ajwain, stir over medium heat until it crackles.
- ❖ Add gram flour and stir fry till it emits an aroma. Add the remaining ingredients and stir for a minute.
- ❖ Add the cooked chana and stir until well mixed.
- ❖ Garnished with tomato slices, onion rings, green chillies, lemon and ginger.
- ❖ Serve with bhatura or kulcha.

DAL MAKHANI

(A dish of mixed pulses with a generous topping of butter and cream)

Ingredients

- 1 cup urad dal
- 30 gms chana dal
- 30 gms rajma
- 30 gms ginger-garlic paste
- 400 ml tomato puree
- 1 tsp chilli powder
- ½ cup butter
- ½ cup cream
- Salt to taste

Method

- ❖ Wash and soak the dals for about 3 hours.
- ❖ Boil in 3 litres of water, cook on slow fire till done.
- ❖ Remove the scum that forms the top layer and continue cooking on low heat.
- ❖ Mash the dals with a spoon and add half the butter, ginger-garlic paste, tomato puree, chilli powder and salt.
- ❖ Simmer for an hour stirring frequently.
- ❖ Add the cream and remove from fire.
- ❖ Garnish with remaining butter and serve with tandoori roti.

DAL BUKHARA *(Spicy lentils)*

Ingredients

- 120 gms urad dal (whole)
- 1 cup tomato puree
- 1 tbsp ginger-garlic paste
- 1 cup cream
- 30 gms rajma
- 3 tbsp butter
- 1 tsp chilli powder
- Salt to taste

Method

- ❖ Wash the lentils in running water and soak overnight. Drain.
- ❖ Put the drained lentils in a pot, add salt and water (approximately 1.5 litres), bring to a boil, cover and simmer, until the lentils are cooked and two-thirds of the liquid has evaporated.
- ❖ Mash the lentils against the sides of the pot with a wooden spoon. Add ginger-garlic paste, tomato puree, chilli powder and two tablespoon butter.
- ❖ Stir and cook for 45 minutes, add cream, stir and cook for 10 minutes.
- ❖ Remove into a bowl, garnish with the remaining butter.

DUM BHINDI MASALEWALI

(Lady's fingers cooked in curd and spices)

Ingredients

- 750 gms bhindi
- 300 ml curd
- 1 tbsp garam masala powder
- 2 tbsp pounded red chillies
- 2 tbsp chopped green chillies
- 4 tbsp ginger-garlic paste
- 1 tbsp turmeric powder
- 4 tbsp oil
- 2 tbsp ghee
- Salt to taste

Method

- Blend the curd, garam masala powder, salt, pounded red chillies and half the chopped green chillies.
- Clean and trim the bhindis. Make slant slits with a knife. Soak the bhindis in the curd mixture and keep aside for 10 minutes.
- Heat oil in a pan. Add ginger-garlic paste, green chillies, turmeric powder and fry well. Add the bhindi along with the curd mixture and cook for 10 minutes.
- Top it with ghee and a little garam masala on the bhindi. Cover the pan with a tight fitting lid and place a heavy weight above it. Steam on low heat for 5 minutes. Cook on slow fire till almost dry.
- Garnish with onion rings, tomato slices and serve hot.

Parathas and Rotis

Wheat is the popular cereal in the North. Staple food consists of several types of chapatis *and* rotis. *Although some rice is also consumed, more emphasis is placed on the different types of Indian bread. There are* parathas, puris, naans, kulchas, rotis *and* chapatis *to choose from. Stuffed* parathas *are a speciality of this region.*

LAJAWAB PARATHA

(Paratha stuffed with green peas)

Ingredients

- 1 cup wheat flour
- 1 cup maida
- 1 cup green peas, shelled
- ½ cup coriander leaves
- 1 tbsp mint leaves
- 1 tbsp amchur powder
- ¼ tsp red chilli powder
- 1 green chilli, finely chopped
- 1 tsp chaat masala
- ½ tsp sugar
- 6 tbsp ghee
- Salt to taste

Method

- Boil the peas and mash them. Add a little salt, chaat masala and chilli powder. Mix well and keep aside.
- Grind together the mint leaves, coriander leaves and green chillies into a fine paste. Add the amchur powder, salt and sugar to this paste to form a chutney.
- Sift the flour, add 1 tbsp of ghee and a little salt and knead with the green chutney to form a stiff dough.
- Divide this into equal portions, and form balls.
- Make a cup in the centre and fill it with the mashed peas. Seal the edges and roll out into a paratha, taking care that the stuffing does not come out.
- Heat a frying pan and fry the parathas evenly with ghee.

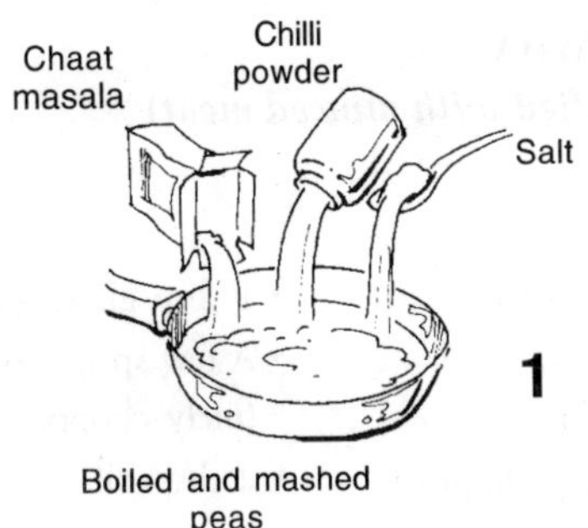
Chaat masala
Chilli powder
Salt
1
Boiled and mashed peas

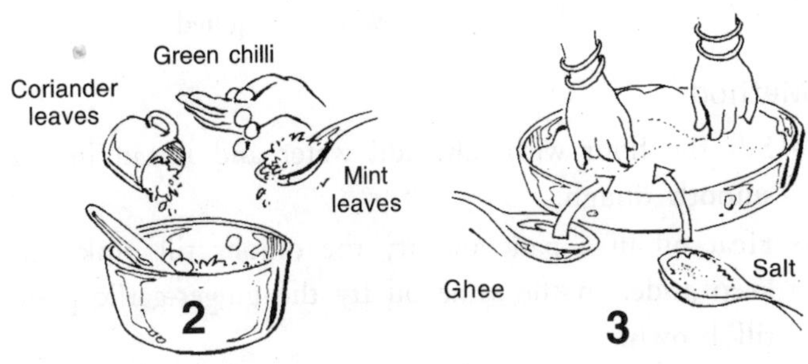
Green chilli
Coriander leaves
Mint leaves
2
Ghee
Salt
3

Mashed peas
4

5

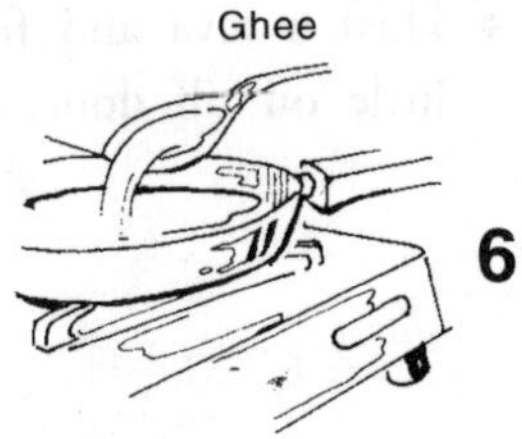
Ghee
6

SHAHI PARATHA

(Paratha stuffed with minced meat)

Ingredients

- 1 cup wheat flour
- 500 gms keema
- 2 eggs, beaten
- 1 onion, finely chopped
- 1 tomato, finely chopped
- 5 green chillies, finely chopped
- 1 tbsp ginger-garlic paste
- A few sprigs coriander leaves, finely chopped
- 2 tbsp oil
- 2 tbsp ghee
- Salt and red chilli powder to taste
- Water as required

Method

- ❖ Sift the flour with salt, add water and knead into a smooth dough.
- ❖ Heat oil in a pan, and fry the onions till pink and keep aside. In the same oil fry the ginger-garlic paste till brown.
- ❖ Add keema, salt and red chilli powder, ½ cup water and cook on low flame till the meat is cooked and dry.
- ❖ Add the tomato to the beaten eggs. Add salt and fry to make two omelettes, keep aside.
- ❖ Take two portions from the prepared dough and roll out into thin chapatis.
- ❖ On one chapati place one omelette, spread a tablespoon of the keema over the omelette, sprinkle some green chillies and coriander leaves and cover with the other omelette.
- ❖ Top this with the other chapati and press the edges of the two chapatis tightly.
- ❖ Heat a tava and fry the paratha on both sides in a little oil till done. Serve hot.

NAAN ***(Fermented Indian bread)***

Ingredients

- 250 gms maida
- 125 ml milk
- ¼ cup butter
- 1 tbsp sugar
- 30 gms yeast
- ½ tbsp salt
- ½ tbsp baking powder
- 1 tbsp poppy seeds

Method

- ❖ In a large mixing bowl, sift together the flour, baking powder, salt and sugar.
- ❖ Blend the yeast with 2 tablespoon of milk. Warm the remaining milk and add to the yeast with 1½ tablespoon of butter. Mix well.
- ❖ Make a hollow in the centre of the maida and gradually pour the yeast mixture. Knead well until the dough is smooth and springy.
- ❖ Cover with a cloth, and leave to rise for about 2 hours at room temperature.
- ❖ Divide the dough into 8 portions and roll out each into a ball with floured hands. Cover the dough balls with a cloth and leave for about 15 minutes.
- ❖ Flatten each ball into circles of about 5 inches in diameter. Brush the tops with melted butter and sprinkle with poppy seeds.
- ❖ Place the dough circles on a greased baking tray and bake at 230°C for about 10 minutes until the naan is puffed up. Serve hot.

MUGHLAI PARATHA

(Paratha with egg coating)

Ingredients

- 250 gms wheat flour
- 2 eggs
- 6 tbsp oil
- 1 tsp baking powder
- Salt to taste

Method

- Sieve together flour, salt and baking powder. Rub the flour with 2 tablespoon oil and slowly add water to make a stiff dough.
- Divide the dough into 8 equal portions and shape them into round balls. Roll out each into a thick flat round. Apply a little oil, sprinkle a little flour and fold it into a semicircle. Again apply oil and flour. Fold it lengthwise. Roll it, press down and roll out into a square of 8" x 8".
- Brush the surface of each paratha with beaten eggs and turn all four corners towards the centre.
- Heat griddle and apply oil liberally. Put the paratha on it. Cook by adding oil around the edges. Turn and fry the other side by applying oil. When brown patches appear on both sides, remove from the griddle. Serve hot.

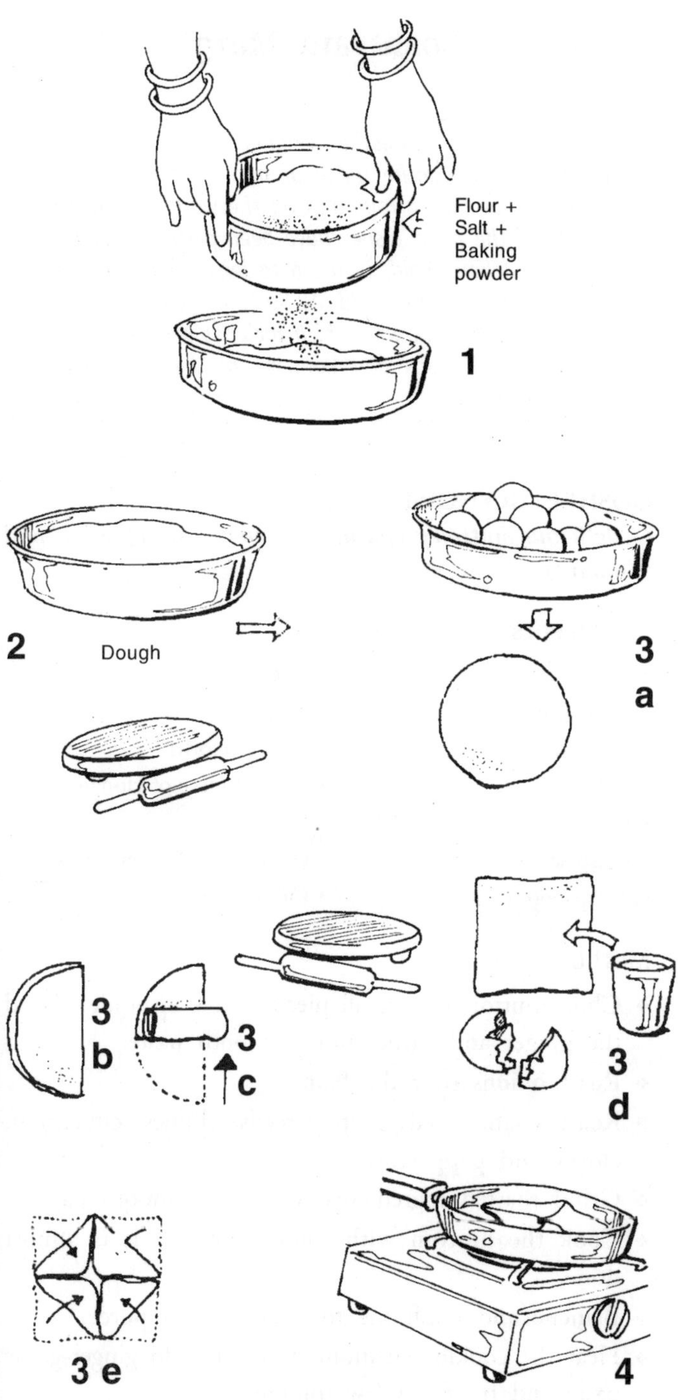
Flour +
Salt +
Baking
powder
1
2
Dough
3
a
3
b
3
c
3
d
3 e
4

Gosht aur Murg

Like it was mentioned earlier, Mughlai *as well as* Kashmiri *cooking have an entire range of non-vegetarian delights which have become a rage all over the world. The distinct flavours of the meat dishes have been perfected by chefs of the royal household, in a bid to lend them a place of honour in the culinary world. All* Kashmiri *feasts worth the name must have* Wazwan *which includes several types of meat dishes.* Kababs *and* kormas *are the speciality of* Mughlai *cooking.*

GOSHT-E-LUCKNOWI

(A delicious mutton preparation from the city of 'adab' and 'shayari')

Ingredients

- ½ kg mutton
- 4 tomatoes
- 2 onions
- 3 cloves garlic
- 1" piece of ginger
- ½ tsp sesame seeds
- ½ tsp poppy seeds
- 4 red chillies
- 3 cloves
- 4 peppercorns
- A small piece of cinnamon
- Salt to taste
- Chopped coriander leaves
- Oil for frying

Method

- Chop mutton into small pieces and keep aside. Grind the ginger and garlic into a smooth paste.
- Roast onions over the flame.
- Roast sesame seeds, poppy seeds, chillies, cinnamon, cloves and peppercorns.
- Grind roasted ingredients to form a smooth paste.
- Cook the mutton with some water till it is almost done.
- Blanche and mash the tomatoes into a puree.
- Heat the cooking medium in a pan, add ginger-garlic paste and fry for a few minutes.

- Add the cooked meat with the ground masala and fry until all the moisture dries and the colour changes to a reddish brown.
- Add tomato puree and salt and continue to simmer on a low flame for about five minutes.
- Garnish with chopped coriander leaves and a dash of fresh cream.

MUTTON LENTIL-DO-PYAAZA

(This is one of the oldest and commonest mutton curries made in the northern parts of the country. A proper do-pyaaza has no gravy save that of ghee and masalas)

Ingredients

- ½ kg mutton
- 225 gms onion
- 225 gms lentils
- 2 cloves of garlic
- ½ tsp cumin seeds
- 5 gms red chilli powder
- 55 gms curd
- 55 gms ghee
- 6 peppercorns
- ½ tsp turmeric powder
- Salt to taste

Method

- Wash and cut the meat into 5 cm pieces.
- Crush well half the onion, garlic and cumin. Grind red chillies to a paste.
- Mix with salt and curd. Rub this curd mixture well into the meat and leave for half an hour.
- Heat ghee and fry the remaining onion slices.
- Add meat. Cover the pan and shake well.
- Add lentils and enough water to cover them.
- Cook over medium heat. Add crushed peppercorns and turmeric powder.
- Simmer till all the water has evaporated and the meat has been cooked.
- Garnish with coriander leaves.

GOSHT-E-DILRUBA *(Meat with vegetables)*

Ingredients

- 400 gms lamb meat
- 250 gms colocasia
- 2 medium-sized potatoes
- 200 gms peas, shelled
- 2 medium-sized onions, chopped
- 2 tsp ginger-garlic paste
- 2 green chillies
- ½ tsp kasuri methi
- 1 tsp red chilli powder
- 100 ml tomato puree
- 1tbsp ajwain
- 1 bay leaf
- Salt to taste
- Coriander leaves for garnishing

Method

- ❖ Boil the peas,colocasia and potatoes till they are half cooked. Cut into thin slices.
- ❖ Heat the oil and fry the slices till they are light brown. Keep aside.
- ❖ In a pan, heat 1 tablespoon oil and add half of the ginger-garlic paste, green chillies, bay leaf and kasuri methi. Fry for 2 minutes. Add tomato puree and fry till the oil floats on top. Keep aside. This is for the gravy.
- ❖ Heat 2 tbsp oil and add ajwain. Add the chopped onion and fry till light brown. Add the remaining ginger-garlic paste and the meat. Sauté for about 5 minutes. Sprinkle some water and cook till done. Add the vegetables, salt and chilli powder and mix lightly.
- ❖ Pour the tomato gravy and fry for 2 more minutes.
- ❖ Garnish with coriander leaves and serve hot with naan or parathas.

MASALA GOSHT *(Spicy, fried meat dish)*

Ingredients

- ½ kg meat
- 1 large onion
- 1 tbsp ginger-garlic paste
- 300 ml curd
- 6 peppercorns
- 4 cloves
- 3" piece of cinnamon
- 2 cardamoms
- 3 red chillies
- 1 tsp turmeric powder
- 2 tbsp ghee
- Salt to taste

Method

- Wash and cut the meat into cubes.
- Heat the cooking medium in a pan and add the meat along with other ingredients.
- Seal the pan and cook for about 45 minutes without adding any water.
- Open the pan and add 2 teaspoon ghee and fry till the meat is reddish brown in colour.
- Serve hot with rice or roti.

GOSHT-E-AKBARI
(A rich and spicy mutton curry)

Ingredients

For the Gosht

- ½ kg mutton, cubed
- ½ cup milk
- 1 large onion, chopped
- 1 tbsp ginger-garlic paste
- ½ tbsp coriander powder
- 2 tsp chilli powder
- ½ tbsp cumin powder
- 1 tsp garam masala powder
- Salt to taste
- A few strands of saffron dissolved in a tbsp of milk
- 1 tbsp flour
- 1 tbsp ghee

For Seasoning

- 100 gms boiled green peas
- 1 onion, chopped
- 1 tbsp oil
- 2 green cardamoms
- 2 black cardamoms
- 4 cloves
- 1" piece of cinnamon
- 6-8 black peppercorns
- 1 bay leaf
- ½ tbsp shahjeera
- 2 whole red chillies

Method

- Pressure cook the mutton with all the ingredients for the gosht except the saffron, flour and ghee.
- Heat ghee in a pan, add flour and sauté for half a minute.
- Lower the flame and gradually add water. Stir constantly till a smooth batter is obtained.
- Add this batter to the gosht and keep stirring for 5 minutes.
- Add saffron and cook for 5 minutes.
- Heat oil in a vessel and add the whole garam masala, bay leaf and shahjeera. Add the chopped onions and fry till brown.
- Add the green peas and stir for about 2 minutes.
- Add the whole dry red chillies and fry.
- Then add the cooked gosht. Mix well and remove from heat.
- Garnish with onion rings, ginger juliennes, coriander leaves and lemon wedges.

GOSHT LAHORI *(A lamb meat delicacy)*

Ingredients

- 1 kg shoulder of lamb, deboned and cut into 4 cm cubes
- 75 gms desi ghee
- 15 gms coriander seeds, coarsely powdered
- A few coriander leaves, chopped

For the Marinade

- 2½ cups curd, whisked
- 500 gms onions, sliced

- 60 gms ginger, julienned
- 45 gms garlic, chopped fine
- 10 green cardamoms
- 5 cloves
- 2" piece of cinnamon
- 12 black peppercorns
- Salt to taste
- 2 tsp Kashmiri deghi mirch powder

Method

- Mix all the ingredients for the marinade in a large bowl, evenly rub the meat cubes with this marinade and keep aside for two hours.
- Heat ghee in a pan, add the coriander seeds and wait till they sputter.
- Add the meat, along with the marinade. Fry till the liquid comes to a boil.
- Lower the heat, cover and simmer, stirring at regular intervals until meat is almost cooked.
- When the oil floats on top and the gravy is of ketchup consistency, remove from fire.
- Remove in a serving dish, garnish with coriander leaves and serve hot.

SAFED GOSHT

(Mutton cooked in a curd base without the use of any colouring agent)

Ingredients

- ½ kg mutton
- 600 ml curd
- 1 lemon
- 2 tbsp ghee
- Salt to taste

Grind Together

- 8 green chillies
- 6-8 cloves of garlic
- ¼ th coconut
- 1 onion
- 1" piece of ginger
- 1 tbsp poppy seeds
- 1 tbsp Bengal gram
- 1 tbsp coriander seeds
- 1 tbsp coriander leaves
- 2" piece of cinnamon
- 4 cloves

Method

- Wash and cut mutton into cubes.
- Cook meat pieces in salt and curd, on low heat until the meat is tender and the moisture has evaporated.
- Add the ground spices and stir. Cover and cook for another ten minutes.
- Add ghee and fry till the meat turns to a reddish brown colour.
- Add lemon juice and serve hot.

NOOR-E-KOFTA

(Stuffed meat balls in spicy gravy)

Ingredients

For The Kofta

- ½ kg mutton keema
- 4 cloves garlic, chopped
- 2 tbsp roasted gram flour
- 1 tsp garam masala
- ½" piece chopped ginger
- 4 chopped green chillies
- 1½ tbsp thick curd
- 1 tbsp ghee
- 1 tsp cumin powder
- 1 tsp coriander seeds
- ½ tsp ground peppercorns
- ½ tsp cardamom
- A bunch of coriander leaves
- Salt to taste

Kofta Filling

- 1 mashed boiled egg
- 1 tbsp onion (chopped fine)
- 1 tbsp thick cream
- 2 chopped green chillies
- ¼ tsp garam masala powder
- ¼ tsp saffron dissolved in ½ tsp hot milk
- Salt to taste

For The Gravy

- 200 gms onions
- 3 tomatoes, pureed
- 6 cloves of garlic
- 1" piece of ginger
- 5 tbsp ghee
- ½ tsp turmeric powder
- 1 tsp cumin powder
- 1 tsp coriander seeds
- ½ tsp garam masala

Method

- Mix all the ingredients for the filling together. Keep aside.
- Separately mix all the ingredients for the kofta including keema and knead well.
- Divide the kofta mixture into 15 equal portions, flatten each portion and put ¼ teaspoon of the filling mixture into it. Close and roll into smooth balls with wet hands. There should be no cracks in the meat balls.
- For the curry, grind the onion, garlic and ginger.
- Heat 5 tablespoon ghee and fry the ground paste with the rest of the spices till golden brown.
- Gently place the koftas into the curry. Leave to set.
- Turn the koftas carefully and cook over low heat.
- Add tomato puree to the kofta curry. Cover and simmer till the curry thickens. Garnish and serve hot.

HARI MACCHI

(Fish cooked in mint and coriander chutney)

Ingredients

- 1 pomfret (large)
- 2 tsp salt

For The Chutney

- ½ bunch coriander leaves
- ½ bunch mint leaves
- 15 gms pomegranate seeds
- 20 gms green chillies
- 1 tsp garam masala powder
- 1 tsp sugar
- Salt to taste

Method

- Clean pomfret and keep whole.
- Make slits on flat sides and add salt.
- Grind the ingredients for chutney and fill into the slits in the fish, liberally, after washing off the excess salt.
- Grill for 5 minutes on medium flame, on each side.
- Serve hot with onion rings and lemon wedges.

ROGANJOSH (WITH POTATOES)

(A popular meat curry from Kashmir)

Ingredients

- ½ kg leg of mutton
- ½ kg potatoes
- 300 gms onions
- 300 gms tomatoes
- 20 gms coriander seeds
- 60 gms ghee
- 30 gms Kashmiri chillies (seedless)
- 20 gms ginger
- 6-8 cloves of garlic
- A pinch of nutmeg
- A pinch of saffron
- A pinch of mace
- A small piece of ratanjot
- ½ tsp cumin seeds
- Salt to taste

Method

- ❖ Clean and cut meat into 1" pieces.
- ❖ Peel and cut the potatoes into cubes.
- ❖ Chop onions, grind Kashmiri chillies, coriander, ginger, garlic and cumin seeds.
- ❖ Heat ghee. Fry the onions and ground masalas well.
- ❖ Add meat, half the saffron and salt.
- ❖ Fry for about 5 minutes. Add nutmeg, mace and ratanjot.
- ❖ Cook until the meat is tender.
- ❖ When meat is almost done, add potatoes.
- ❖ When the meat and potatoes are cooked, add the rest of the saffron dissolved in a little warm milk.

DUM GOSHT KASHMIRI

(A nutty mutton preparation with spices)

Ingredients

- 1 kg mutton
- 1½" piece of ginger
- 1 pod garlic
- 6 almonds
- 1 tsp peppercorns
- 4 cardamoms
- 3 small sticks of cinnamon
- ½ tsp cumin seeds
- 1 tsp turmeric powder
- 1 tbsp poppy seeds
- A small piece of raw papaya
- A few coriander leaves
- Ghee for frying
- Salt to taste

Method

- ❖ Chop mutton into steak-size pieces.
- ❖ Roast poppy seeds and almonds, and grind to paste.
- ❖ Grind ginger and garlic into a smooth paste.
- ❖ Grind cardamom, peppercorns, papaya and coriander leaves with salt.
- ❖ Wash meat and beat on a grinding stone. Mix ground masala with poppy seed-almond paste, cumin seeds and cinnamon sticks. Marinate the meat pieces in this mixture for an hour.
- ❖ Heat ghee in a frying pan, add the meat pieces and fry for a few minutes. Add 2 cups of water and cook on slow heat till meat is tender.
- ❖ Serve hot, garnished with coriander leaves and lemon slices.

RANN KOHINOORI

(Chunky lamb meat with spices)

Ingredients

- 1 lamb leg (1-1.25 kg)
- 50 gms ginger-garlic paste
- 500 gms beaten curd
- 100 raw papaya, mashed
- 10 gms garam masala powder
- 10 gms chilli powder
- 80 ml mustard oil
- Juice of 1 lemon
- Salt to taste

Method

- ❖ Clean the lamb leg properly and make gashes at various places.
- ❖ Rub in beaten curd, mashed papaya and all the other ingredients and coat thickly.
- ❖ Cover the leg completely with the marinade. Keep it aside for at least 2-3 hours.
- ❖ The cooking of the 'rann' should be done in a thick bottomed pan. Place the leg in the pan, add a litre of water. Seal the lid very tightly with aluminium foil

and cook on slow fire until the water dries up completely and the meat is tender.

- Debone the leg neatly and cut the meat into large chunks.
- Arrange the chunks on a platter along with wedges of lemon, onion rings and coriander leaves.

KARAHI CHICKEN

(Hot and spicy chicken curry)

Ingredients

- 1 chicken, cut into pieces
- 3 medium-sized onions, chopped
- 1½ tsp ginger-garlic paste
- 2 tomatoes, chopped
- 1 tsp Kashmiri red chilli powder
- Whole Kashmiri red chillies
- 1 tsp coriander seeds
- 10 gms garam masala
- 2-3 bay leaves
- 100 ml oil
- ½ bunch coriander leaves, chopped
- Salt to taste

Method

- In a karahi, heat oil, add bay leaves, whole red chillies, coriander seeds, garam masala and roast till they splutter. Add chopped onions and fry till golden brown.
- Add the ginger-garlic paste and fry till the oil floats on top.
- Add chopped tomatoes and cook.
- Add salt, Kashmiri red chilli powder and stir-fry the masala till the oil separates from it. Do not add water.
- Now add the chicken pieces to the masala. Stir and fry the chicken, add a little water for cooking. Remove from fire.
- Sprinkle chopped coriander leaves and garnish with a fried red chilli.

MURG NAWABI

(A delicious chicken preparation fit for the royal palate)

Ingredients

- 1 kg chicken
- 2 medium-sized onions
- 1" piece ginger
- 1½ tsp cumin seeds
- 10 cloves
- 10 cardamoms
- 10 cloves garlic
- 10 peppercorns
- 1½ tsp red chilli powder
- 1" stick cinnamon
- 1 tbsp tomato puree
- 1 tbsp curd
- 1½ tsp coriander powder
- ½ tsp turmeric powder
- 4 tbsp oil
- Salt to taste

Method

- Grind together onion, garlic and ginger.
- Heat oil in a pan. Add the cumin seeds, cardamoms, cinnamon, cloves and peppercorns. Toss in the chicken pieces and fry till brown. Remove from the pan and keep aside.
- In the same pan heat 1 tbsp oil and fry the onion-ginger-garlic paste till light brown.
- Add coriander, turmeric and chilli powder.
- Add curd and tomato puree. Stir for a minute or two. Drop in the browned chicken pieces along with the spices and cook on low heat until the chicken is tender.
- Serve hot with naan or parathas.

TANDOORI MURGH *(Spicy chicken roast)*

Ingredients

- 1 chicken (approx. 750 gm)
- 150 ml curd
- 1 small onion, ground
- 1" ginger, ground
- 6-8 flakes garlic, ground
- 5 tbsp lemon juice
- 1 tsp red chilli powder
- ½ tsp black cumin seeds
- 1 tsp ghee
- Salt to taste

Grind Together

- 4 black peppercorns
- 1 stick cinnamon
- 1 tsp garam masala
- 1 bay leaf
- 2 cloves
- 1 cardamom

Method

- ❖ Mix onion, ginger and garlic with curd.
- ❖ Apply the mixture to the inside as well the outside of the chicken and marinate for 5 hours.
- ❖ Add chilli powder, cumin seeds, salt and ground spices to the lemon juice and mix.
- ❖ Make deep gashes with a sharp knife on each side of the chicken and apply the lemon juice mixture. Keep aside for 1 hour.
- ❖ Skewer the chicken, brush it with a little butter and grill on an open charcoal stove or oven for half an hour.
- ❖ Serve hot, sprinkled with garam masala and sliced onion and lemon.

MURG MALAI TIKKA

(A dish of succulent tikkas from the tenderest of the chicken meat)

Ingredients

- 12 nos. chicken breasts or legs
- 1 egg
- 100 gms processed cheese
- 8 green chillies
- 20 gms green coriander
- 80 ml cream
- 15 gms cornflour
- 80 gms ginger-garlic paste
- 60 ml lemon juice
- 1 tsp white pepper powder
- Salt to taste

For Garnishing

- Onion rings
- Coriander leaves
- Tomato slices
- Green chillies
- Lemon wedges
- Chaat masala powder

Method

- ❖ Cut the chicken breasts/legs into 2 pieces each.
- ❖ Add the ginger-garlic paste, salt, white pepper powder, and lemon juice.
- ❖ Rub well and keep aside for ten minutes.
- ❖ Break the egg in a bowl. Clean, wash and finely chop the coriander leaves and de-seed the chillies.
- ❖ Mix the cheese, green chillies, coriander, cream, cornflour and egg into a smooth marinade.
- ❖ Squeeze out the excess moisture from the chicken pieces, and rub them with the cheese mixture. Keep aside for 40 minutes.
- ❖ Skewer the chicken pieces and roast on a moderately hot tandoor for approximately 5 minutes.
- ❖ Remove and hang skewers for a few seconds so that the excess moisture drips off.
- ❖ Baste with butter and roast again for 5-6 minutes. Remove from the skewers.
- ❖ Pre-heat the oven to 300° F. Cook the kababs for about 5 minutes.
- ❖ Arrange the chicken tikkas on a platter and garnish with the onion rings, lemon wedges, tomato pieces, coriander leaves, sprinkle the chaat masala and serve.

MURG LAJAWAB *(Boneless chicken in cream)*

Ingredients

- 800 gms boneless chicken
- 200 ml cream
- 50 gms grated cheese
- 2 eggs
- 10 gms green chillies
- 50 gms cornflour
- 25 gms ginger
- 10 gms cardamom, powdered
- 5 gms mace powder
- Salt to taste

Method

- Clean, wash and cut the chicken into medium-sized pieces.
- Make a marinade of cream, cheese, eggs and cornflour.
- Add the chicken pieces, chopped green chillies, chopped ginger and salt.
- Mix in the spices and set aside for 4-6 hours.
- Skewer the chicken pieces on a 'seekh' and roast in a moderately hot tandoor, for 8-10 minutes, basting it with oil from time to time.
- Serve hot, garnished with onion rings and lemon wedges.

MURG-ANARKALI *(A hot and spicy chicken dish)*

Ingredients

- 1 chicken
- 1 cup onion paste
- 1 chopped onion
- 20 dried red chillies
- 2 tsp ginger-garlic paste
- 5-6 green chillies
- 1 cup curd
- 2 green peppers
- 5-6 green cardamoms
- 5-6 black cardamoms
- 5-6 bay leaves
- 2 tbsp mixed garam masala (cloves, cinnamon, cumin seeds)
- 1 tbsp whole black peppers
- 1 ½ tsp mace
- ¼ tsp nutmeg paste
- 5 tbsp oil
- 1 small piece ratanjot
- ¼ tsp turmeric powder
- 2½ tsp coriander powder
- Salt to taste

Method

- Mix salt with curd and pour over the chicken pieces. Chop the green peppers.
- Heat oil and add the pepper pieces and fry lightly. Remove from the oil, add red chillies and bay leaves.
- Add whole dry spices and ratanjot. When ratanjot has left its red colour, remove it from the oil. Add chopped onions and fry till it turns light brown in colour.
- Add all the pastes, fry well.

- Add turmeric powder and coriander powder, sprinkle 2 tablespoon water and fry the masala. Add chicken pieces with curd, fry pieces with masala mixture till all the moisture dries out.
- Add 1 cup water, green chillies and the peppers. Cover and cook till done.
- Serve hot with naan or paratha.

MURG MAKHANI *(Roasted chicken in a cream base)*

Ingredients

- 1 kg tandoori chicken
- ½ kg tomatoes, chopped
- 50 gms butter
- ½ cup cream
- ½ cup water
- 4 tbsp cashewnuts
- 3 bay leaves
- ½ tsp chilli powder
- ½ tsp garam masala powder
- 1 tsp sugar
- 2 green chillies, finely chopped
- Coriander leaves for garnishing
- Salt to taste

Method

- Make tomato puree by boiling it with the bay leaves for 5 minutes. Blend in the mixie, when cool. Sieve it and keep aside.
- Grind the cashewnuts into a fine powder.
- Heat butter in a pan and fry the cashew powder till golden brown in colour. Lower the heat and add the tomato puree, chilli powder, garam masala powder and sugar.
- Simmer for ten minutes. Add the tandoori chicken and cook for 5 minutes.
- Garnish with onion rings, coriander leaves, green chillies and cream.
- Serve hot with naan.

PRAWN CAPSICUM BALLS
(Capsicums with prawn filling)

Ingredients

- 400 gms capsicums
- 400 prawns, shelled
- 2 large onions, finely minced
- 1" piece of ginger
- 1 pod garlic
- 1 tsp peppercorns
- 1 tsp coriander seeds
- 1 tsp cumin seeds
- 1 tsp aniseeds
- 2 sticks of cinnamon
- 6 cloves
- 4 green chillies
- 2 eggs
- 1tsp gramflour
- Bread crumbs
- 3 tbsp ghee
- 2 large tomatoes, chopped
- ½ tsp turmeric powder
- Salt to taste

Method

- Slice the tops of capsicum, keep the stalks aside. Scoop the inner contents and wash.
- Apply salt and keep upside down on a rack.
- Devein the prawns and mince them fine.
- Heat ghee, fry the finely minced onions to light brown.
- Grind the ginger, garlic and other masalas to a fine paste.
- Add this to the onions, fry well and add the prawn mince.
- Lastly add tomatoes, fry into a dry paste and add finely chopped coriander leaves.
- Fill this mixture into the capsicums, attach the stalks and seal well with gramflour.
- Now dip in beaten egg and roll in bread crumbs and deep fry to a golden brown colour.
- Serve hot with sauce.

DILBAHAR FISH TIKKA *(Spicy fish fillets)*

Ingredients

- 500 gms pomfret fillets
- 2 tbsp gramflour
- 1 tsp ginger-garlic paste
- 1 tsp chilli powder
- 4 tbsp curd
- 1 tsp white vinegar
- 2 tbsp thick cream
- A pinch of nutmeg powder
- 3 green cardamoms, crushed
- Chaat masala to taste
- Salt to taste

Method

- ❖ Clean and wash fish.
- ❖ Cut into thick pieces, apply salt and vinegar and keep aside for 15 minutes.
- ❖ Pat dry. Mix together all the ingredients and apply to the fish pieces.
- ❖ Marinate for half an hour. Bake in a hot oven for 15 minutes.
- ❖ Sprinkle chaat masala and serve hot with mint chutney.

SAMUDRI TOOFAN
(A spicy grilled fish preparation)

Ingredients

- 1 large pomfret, cut into pieces
- 1 tbsp lemon juice
- Salt

Grind For The Marinade

- 1½ tsp red pepper (deghi mirchi)
- 2 cloves of garlic
- 1 tsp coriander seeds
- 15 ml vinegar
- ¼ tsp amchur powder
- 2 tsp lemon juice
- A pinch of fenugreek seeds
- 8 gms ginger

For The Seasoning

- ½ tbsp cumin seeds
- 2 tbsp amchur powder
- 1 tbsp ghee
- Salt to taste

Method

- ❖ Wash and dry the fish. Make slits all over. Rub in the lemon juice and salt. Keep aside for an hour.
- ❖ Rub the marinade paste into the fish pieces and marinate for two hours.
- ❖ Grill in an oven for 10-15 minutes.
- ❖ Season and serve hot, accompanied by chopped onions and slit green chillies.

TOMATO MACHHI *(Fish cooked in a tomato base)*

Ingredients

- ½ kg fish fillets
- 4 tomatoes
- 100 ml curd
- 35 gm garlic paste
- 1tbsp ginger juliennes
- 1 tbsp gramflour
- 5 green chillies, chopped fine
- 1 tsp garam masala powder
- 1 tbsp chilli powder
- Few coriander leaves, chopped
- 3 tbsp oil
- ½ tsp turmeric powder
- 1 tsp cumin seeds
- 4 cloves
- 4 cardamoms
- Salt to taste

Method

- ❖ Wash the fish fillets with gramflour. Blend the tomatoes in a mixie. Strain and keep the puree aside.
- ❖ Whisk the curd in the mixie and keep aside.
- ❖ Grind the garlic to a paste. Mix the beaten curd, garlic paste, salt, garam masala powder, green chillies, half the coriander leaves and chilli powder.
- ❖ Marinate the fish fillets in this mixture for 30 minutes.
- ❖ Heat oil in a pan, add ginger juliennes, turmeric powder, cumin seeds, cloves and cardamom. Fry for a minute, add tomato puree and keep stirring for 5 minutes.
- ❖ Add the marinated fish and cook for 10 minutes or till both sides are done.
- ❖ Garnish with remaining coriander leaves and serve hot with rice.

MUTTON-ALOO-PALAK

(Mutton curry with spinach and potatoes)

Ingredients

- ½ kg mutton
- ½ kg potatoes
- ½ kg spinach
- 115 gms onions
- 4 cloves of garlic
- 15 gm ginger
- ½ tsp cumin seeds
- ½ tsp turmeric powder
- 5 gms red chillies
- 5 gm green chillies
- Salt to taste
- Oil for cooking

Method

- Wash and cut the mutton into even portions. Peel and cut the potatoes.
- Grind red chillies, ginger, garlic and cumin seeds. Slice the onions.
- Heat the oil and fry the sliced onions till light brown.
- Add ground masala and fry till the oil floats on top.
- Add meat and a little water and cook until the meat is almost cooked.
- Wash and chop the spinach and cook without water.
- Grind the palak and add to the meat.
- When the meat is three-fourth done, add potatoes.
- Cook until the meat and potatoes are tender.
- Garnish with coriander leaves and serve hot.

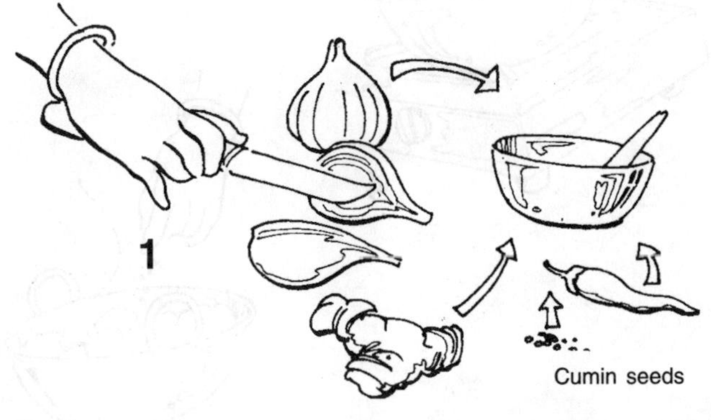

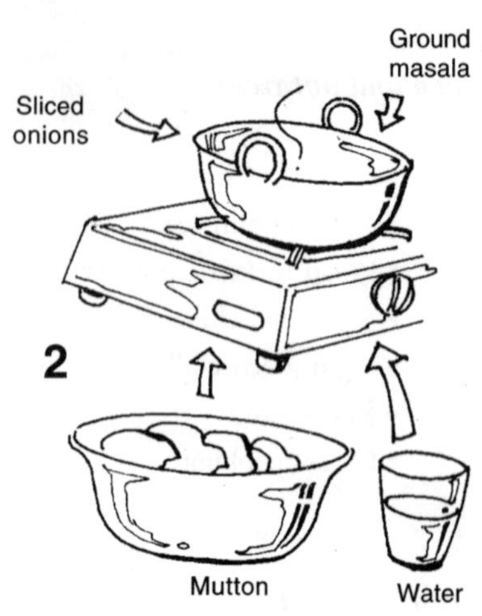

3

Ground
palak

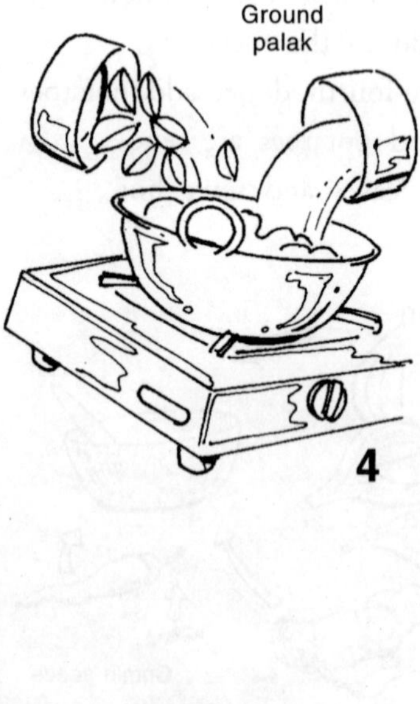

4

5

Biryani and Pulao

No dawat *in the North can be complete without the inclusion of* biryanis *and* pulaos. *The* biryanis *were cooked in* handis *under* dum, *in the Mughal era. The earthenware lends the* biryani *a distinctive flavour, which cannot be duplicated in modern-day utensils. Both meat as well as chicken can be used in the preparation of a* biryani. *There are vegetarian* biryanis *and* pulaos *for those who do not enjoy the non-vegetarian fare.*

MURG DUM BIRYANI *(Chicken biryani)*

Ingredients

- 750 gms chicken, cut into 8 pieces
- 350 gms basmati rice, washed and soaked for 20 minutes
- 120 gms ghee
- 1 tsp whole garam masala
- ½ tsp shahjeera
- 150 gms onions, sliced
- 150 ml curd
- 70 gms ginger-garlic paste
- 2 tsp chilli powder
- 40 ml lemon juice
- 50 ml cream
- 25 gms browned onion
- 25 gms mint leaves,
- 25 gms coriander leaves, chopped chopped
- A few strands saffron, dissolved in a little warm milk
- Salt to taste

Method

- Heat ghee in a pan. Add half of the whole garam masala and shahjeera.
- Saute for a minute, add onions and stir, fry till golden brown.
- Add ginger-garlic paste, salt and chilli powder. Fry, then add chicken.
- Put the curd and saute for two minutes.
- Add about 500 ml of water and bring to a boil. Cover and cook till chicken is almost done. Squeeze the lemon juice on top.

- Boil 1 litre of water in a pan. Add the remaining whole garam masala, salt and rice.
- Cook till the rice is half done, drain out the excess water.
- Place the handi with chicken on low heat.
- Sprinkle half of cream, browned onion, mint leaves, coriander leaves and saffron. Then spread half rice over the chicken.
- Repeat the layers. Place a moist cloth or butter paper on top and seal the lid with dough.
- Put the sealed pan on dum in a pre-heated oven for 15-20 minutes. Serve hot.

YAKHNI BIRYANI

(Mutton biryani cooked with whole garam masala)

Ingredients

- 350 gms basmati rice, washed and soaked for 30 minutes
- 5 tsp lemon juice
- 8 cloves
- 6 cardamoms
- 2" cinnamon stick
- Salt to taste

For The Yakhni

- 400 gms mutton, cubed
- 200 gms onions, chopped fine
- 50 gms onions, sliced and browned (for garnishing)
- 200 ml curd
- 25 gms ghee
- 25 gms ginger-garlic paste
- 10 gms ginger, julienned
- 1 tsp whole garam masala
- ¼ tsp cardamom-mace powder
- ½ tsp pepper powder
- A few mint leaves, chopped
- Salt to taste

Method

- Heat ghee and season with the whole garam masala.
- Add the chopped onion and fry till golden brown. Add the mutton and the ginger-garlic paste and sauté for 5 minutes. Add curd and fry for 5 minutes.
- Add the remaining ingredients and fry for 2 minutes.

- ❖ Add enough water and cook till the meat is tender.
- ❖ Boil 1 litre water with salt, cinnamon, cardamom, cloves and lemon juice. Add the rice and cook till half done and drain out the excess water.
- ❖ Take the handi with yakhni and put it on low fire so that it is hot. Sprinkle a few chopped mint leaves, and spread the rice on top. Cover with a moist cloth and seal the lid with dough. Put the sealed handi on dum with live charcoal on top for 10-15 minutes. Garnish with browned onions. Serve hot, with raita.

MATAR PULAO *(Green pea pulao)*

Ingredients

- 500 gms basmati rice
- 1 large onion, sliced
- 2 cups green peas, parboiled
- 170 gms ghee
- 1 bay leaf
- 7-8 peppercorns
- 3" cinnamon stick
- 2 cardamoms
- 7-8 cloves
- A handful of cashewnuts
- 100 gms of raisins
- Salt to taste

Method

- ❖ Wash the rice and soak it for half an hour. Drain off the excess water.
- ❖ In a pan heat the ghee and add the sliced onions and fry till they are light brown in colour.
- ❖ Fry the cashewnuts and raisins and keep aside.
- ❖ Add cloves, cinnamon, peppercorns and cardamoms and fry for a minute and add the rice. Fry on low heat so that each grain of rice is coated with ghee.
- ❖ Add the peas and fry for 3 minutes.
- ❖ Add salt and cover the rice with double the amount of boiling water.
- ❖ Bring to a boil and simmer with the closed lid till the rice is done and the water has been absorbed.
- ❖ Garnish with fried cashewnuts and raisins and serve hot.

MANPASAND BIRYANI *(Spiced chicken biryani)*

Ingredients

- 600 gms chicken
- 600 gms basmati rice, parboiled
- ½ cup ghee
- 250 gms tomatoes, sliced
- 8 green chillies
- Coriander leaves
- 5 tsp lime juice
- 180 ml milk
- 75 gms onion slices, fried

For The Marinade

- 2½ cups curd
- 2 tbsp ginger-garlic paste
- 1 tbsp chilli powder
- 1 tbsp garam masala powder
- 1 tbsp almond powder
- 3 potatoes, cubed and fried
- ½ tsp turmeric powder
- Green chillies, slit
- Coriander leaves, chopped
- A few strands of saffron
- Salt to taste

For Tempering

- 2 bay leaves
- 2 petals mace
- 2 cardamoms
- 2 cloves
- 2" piece of cinnamon

Method

- ❖ Marinate the chicken with the marinade mixture for 30 minutes.
- ❖ Heat ghee. Add the tempering and fry for a minute. Add the parboiled rice, stir lightly and keep aside.
- ❖ Line a heavy bottom pan with double foil. Arrange thickly sliced tomatoes to cover the base. Place the marinated chicken over it. Arrange green chillies and 2/3rd of the rice over it.
- ❖ Sprinkle coriander leaves, fried onion slices, lime juice and milk. Top with the rest of the rice.
- ❖ Pour the ghee and seal the pan and cook on medium heat for 35 minutes.
- ❖ Serve hot with raita.

PUDINA PULAO *(Mint flavoured vegetarian pulao)*

Ingredients

- 1 cup basmati rice (washed and soaked for 30 minutes)
- 2 large onions, chopped fine
- 2 tbsp ghee
- 1 tsp cumin seeds
- 50 gms pudina leaves
- Salt to taste

For Seasoning

- 4 cloves
- 6 peppercorns
- 2 cardamoms
- 1" piece of cinnamon
- 2 bay leaves

Method

- Heat ghee in a pressure pan, add the whole garam masala and cumin seeds and fry for a minute.
- Add onions and fry for about 4 minutes.
- Add the soaked rice and fry for 5 minutes on low heat. Add salt, 2 cups water and mint leaves.
- Pressure cook for one whistle and switch off the gas.
- Open the pressure pan and sprinkle lime juice over the pulao.
- Serve hot with raita or plain curd.

PANCHRANGI PULAO *(Mixed vegetable pulao)*

Ingredients

- 350 gms basmati rice, washed and soaked for 20 minutes
- 120 gms ghee
- 100 gms onions, chopped fine
- 100 gms potatoes, cubes
- 100 gms carrots, cubed
- 100 gms French beans, diced
- 75 gms green peas, shelled
- 100 gms white pumpkin, cubed
- 8 green chillies, split lengthwise
- 50 gms ginger-garlic paste
- 10 gms chilli powder
- 1" ginger cut into juliennes
- 5 gms whole garam masala
- A few strands of saffron soaked in a little warm milk
- 20 gms chopped mint leaves
- 20 gms chopped coriander leaves
- A pinch of cardamom/mace powder
- Salt to taste

Method

- Heat a little ghee in a pan.
- Add half the garam masala, sauté till it begins to crackle.
- Add the onions and brown them. Add half of the green chillies, ginger-garlic paste, chilli powder and salt. Sauté for 5 minutes.
- Add the vegetables, stir for a while till they are well coated with the masala. Add enough water and cook till done.
- Bring about 1 litre of water to boil, add salt and the remaining whole garam masala. Add rice and cook till half done.
- Drain out the excess water.
- Take the pan with the cooked vegetables and sprinkle half of the ginger juliennes, green chillies, half of saffron milk, mint leaves and coriander leaves. Spread half of the rice over the vegetables.
- Repeat the layer. Place a moist cloth on top. Cover with a lid and seal with dough.
- Put the sealed handi on dum (on low heat) or in a pre-heated oven, for 10-15 minutes. Serve hot with raita.

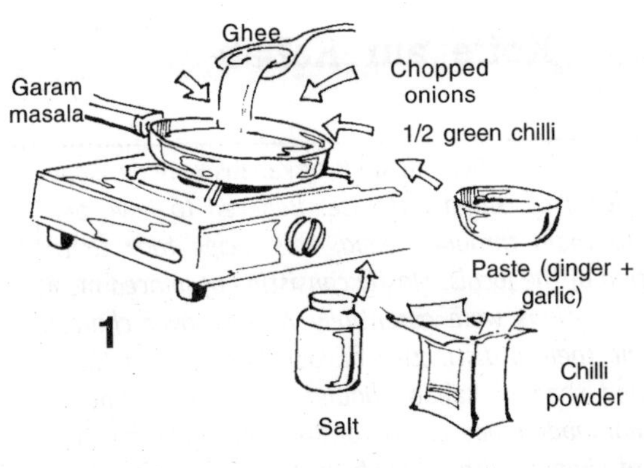
Ghee
Garam masala
Chopped onions
1/2 green chilli
Paste (ginger + garlic)
Salt
Chilli powder
1

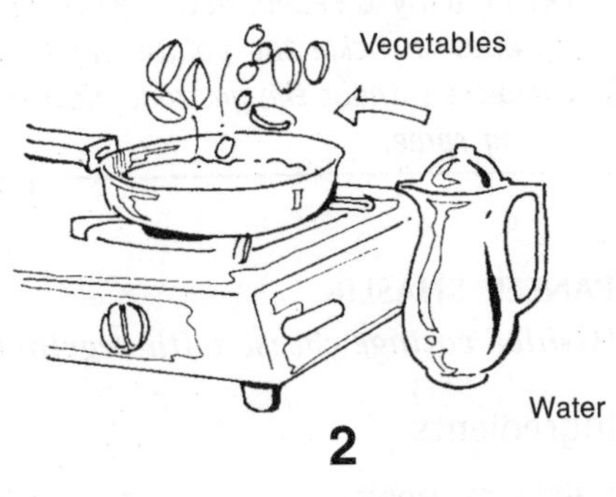
Vegetables
Water
2

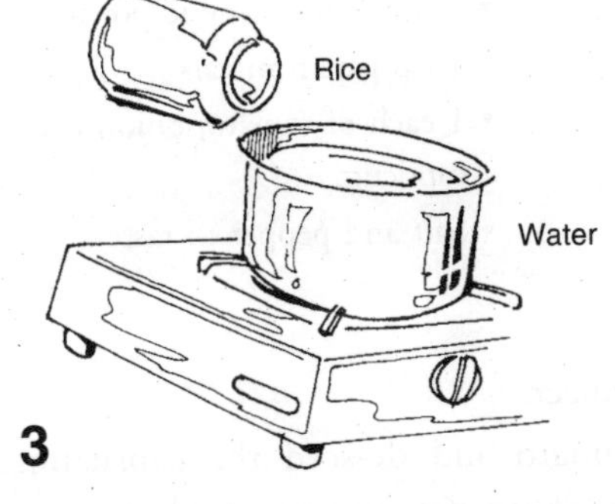
Rice
Water
3

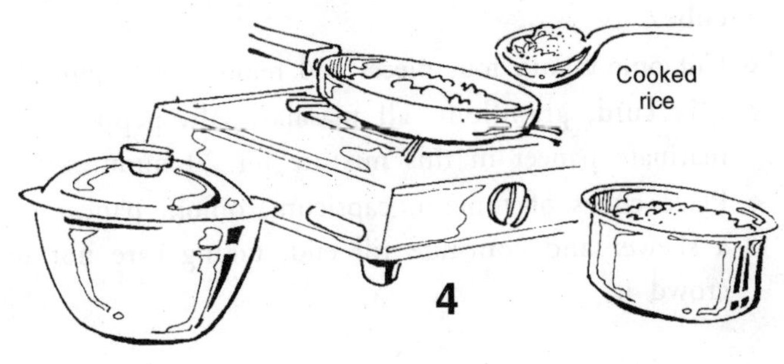
Cooked rice
4

Kofte aur Kabab

North was the place where all kinds of kababs *were developed to the heights of culinary finesse. Believed to have been brought to India through Persia, this recipe took to the imagination of the locals. Mostly consisting of minced meat, these preparations were essentially roasted over charcoal fire to lend them a distinctive flavour. Popular varieties of* sheekh *and* shammi kabab *abound in almost all menus. The popular modern day version of* Roomali *roti with* kababs *is a roll of chapati with a* kabab *in it.* Nargisi kofta, kathi kabab, hariyali kabab, pathar kabab, *there are innumerable varieties to tickle the palate. No trip to Lucknow is ever complete without the gastronomical indulgence of a* kabab *eating spree.*

PANEER SHASLIK

(Grilled cottage cheese with vegetables)

Ingredients

- 400 gms paneer
- 100 gms curd
- 30 gms gramflour
- 1 tsp coriander powder
- 1 tsp cumin powder
- 1 pinch of turmeric powder
- 1 tsp garam masala
- 1 each of tomato, onion and capsicum
- Salt and pepper to taste

Method

- Cut 2" cubes of paneer.
- Remove pulp of tomato and de-seed the capsicum. Cut them into cubes, about the same size as the paneer cubes.
- Cut onions into four pieces and remove the segments.
- Mix curd, gramflour, all masalas, salt, pepper and marinate paneer in this mixture for 20 minutes.
- Place cubes of tomato, capsicum, onion, paneer on a skewer and continue till end, taking care not to crowd it.

- Brush with oil and grill on medium heat for 10 minutes.
- Take out the shaslik and decorate with onion rings, lemon wedges on a platter and serve hot.

HARA KABAB ***(A vegetarian kabab)***

Ingredients

- 250 gms paneer
- 50 gms palak puree
- 60 gms cornflour
- 1 tsp garam masala
- 1 tsp chilli powder
- 1 tbsp pepper powder
- 1 tsp coriander powder
- Salt to taste

Method

- Grate paneer and mix with palak puree.
- Add salt, pepper, garam masala and other powdered masalas.
- Add cornflour, mix well.
- Divide into even-sized balls and grill in the oven, basting with oil, frequently.
- Serve with onion rings, and mint chutney.

SHEEKH KABAB
(Keema skewered and roasted on charcoal)

Ingredients

- ½ kg mutton keema
- 1 tsp chilli powder
- ¼ tsp tenderised, crushed raw papaya
- ½ tsp garam masala
- ½ tsp shahjeera powder
- ¼ tsp nutmeg powder
- 1 egg yolk
- 1 tsp kasuri methi powder
- 1 tsp cornflour or gramflour
- 1 tsp poppy seeds, powdered
- 2 tsp cashewnuts, powdered
- ½ red colouring powder
- 1 tsp crushed ginger
- ½ tsp crushed garlic
- 1 tbsp each crushed onions, green chillies and coriander leaves
- Salt to taste

Method

- ❖ Add tenderised papaya to mince meat and leave in the fridge for half an hour.
- ❖ Mix all ingredients except egg yolk, to the minced meat mixture and blend in the mixie till a fine paste is obtained.
- ❖ Add egg yolk and mix well. Refrigerate for one hour.
- ❖ Divide the mixture into 12 portions. Shape into sausage like cylinders and place on the skewers. Use a little water to hold the kabab mixture on the skewers.
- ❖ Roast on charcoal or on the grill.
- ❖ While roasting, brush with butter once or twice.
- ❖ Serve hot with mint chutney.

HUSSAINI KABAB

(This kabab is different by the virtue of having coconut as one of its ingredients)

Ingredients

- ½ kg minced mutton
- 4 green chillies, minced
- 1 large onion, minced
- 6 cloves of garlic, minced
- 1" piece ginger, minced
- 1 tsp dessicated coconut
- 6 almonds
- 1 tsp gramflour
- 1 tsp coriander powder
- 1 tsp turmeric powder
- 1 tsp garam masala
- 2 tsp lime juice
- Oil for frying
- Salt to taste

Method

- ❖ Mix all the ingredients thoroughly and heat on low fire for 10-15 minutes.
- ❖ Cool, grind to a fine paste, adding 2 tsp lime juice.
- ❖ Shape into oval-shaped kababs and deep fry until golden brown.
- ❖ Serve hot with mint chutney.

MINT MUTTON CHOPS

(Chops with a mint flavour)

Ingredients

- 500 gms mutton chops
- ½ cup curd, lightly whipped
- 2 tomatoes
- 2 onions
- 8-10 cloves of garlic
- 2" piece of ginger
- 2-3 green chillies
- 20 mint leaves
- 1 tbsp coriander leaves, finely chopped
- 5 cloves
- ½ tbsp pepper powder
- ½ tbsp garam masala powder
- ½ tsp turmeric powder
- 8-10 almonds, sliced
- A handful of cashewnuts, chopped
- 2 tbsp ghee
- 2 tbsp butter
- 2 tbsp cream
- Salt to taste

For Decoration

- 1 capsicum
- 1 tomato
- 1 onion
- 5 almonds
- 5 cashewnuts

Method

- Wash and drain the chops. Grind ginger, garlic, mint leaves, coriander leaves, green chillies, pepper, tomatoes, cloves, to a fine paste.
- Add curd, salt and turmeric powder to this paste. Apply the paste to the meat chops.
- Allow the chops to marinate for half an hour.
- Heat ghee and fry the onions. Add the marinated chops and fry well.
- Pressure cook till tender and done.
- Open and fry till almost dry.
- Slice the capsicum, tomato and onions into rings.
- Heat a little butter and fry these slices. Keep aside.
- Grease a baking dish, arrange the cooked chops in it and decorate with the capsicum, onion and tomato rings. Pour cream over the sliced vegetables.

- Garnish with salt, pepper, almonds and cashewnut pieces.
- Bake in a pre-heated oven on moderate heat for 20 minutes.
- Serve hot with roomali roti.

KASHMIRI KABAB

(Predominantly populated by Muslims, Kashmir is a place where the recipes for various meat preparations were honed to perfection. The kababs find a place of honour in their ritualistic Wazwan feasts)

Ingredients

- 1 kg mutton, minced
- 2 onions, quartered
- 4 green chillies, cut in big pieces
- 1½" piece of ginger
- 1 raw egg
- 1½ tsp red chilli powder
- 1 tbsp jeera powder, roasted
- Salt and pepper to taste

Method

- Clean and wash the keema.
- Mix all ingredients except raw egg.
- Add the raw egg and blend it well. Shape this mixture into oblong pieces like sheekh kabab.
- Boil 2 glasses of water in a shallow pan. While the water is boiling, gently slide the kababs in it. Let the kababs simmer till the entire water evaporates.
- Deep fry kababs in a shallow pan till light brown.
- Serve hot with lemon wedges and onion slices.

JHINGA KABAB *(Prawn kabab)*

Ingredients

- 500 gms prawns
- 1 egg
- 2 cups fresh green chana, boiled and mashed
- 3 medium-sized onions, chopped
- 8-10 cloves garlic, chopped
- 10 gms ginger
- 7 green chillies, chopped
- ½ bunch coriander leaves, chopped
- 5 slices bread
- 1 tsp chilli powder
- 1 tsp chaat masala
- 1 tsp garam masala powder
- Salt to taste
- Oil for frying

Method

- Clean, shell and devein the prawns.
- In a wide bowl, mix all the ingredients except oil and egg.
- Lastly beat the egg and blend well into the mixture.
- Shape into kababs and deep fry.
- Serve hot.

MAHARANI KOFTA CURRY
(Minced meat balls in a spicy gravy)

Ingredients

For The Koftas

- 1 kg minced meat
- 2 medium-sized onions
- 2½ tbsp gramflour, roasted
- 1 egg
- 2" piece ginger, finely chopped
- 6 green chillies, finely chopped
- 1 tsp red chilli powder
- Salt to taste
- Oil for frying

For Kofta Curry

- 3 medium-sized onions
- 1½" piece ginger
- 3-5 cloves of garlic
- 1 cup tomato puree
- 2 tsp coriander leaves
- 1 tsp turmeric powder
- 1 tsp red chilli powder
- 1 tsp garam masala
- Salt to taste

Method

- Clean the minced meat and refrigerate for half an hour.
- Beat the egg.
- Mix all the ingredients and blend with minced meat and the beaten egg.
- Shape into balls of 1" size.
- Deep fry till golden brown and keep the koftas aside.
- Heat the oil in a pan and fry the onions, ginger, garlic till golden brown.
- Add the rest of the ingredients except coriander, fry for a minute.
- Add sufficient water to make a gravy, bring to a boil and add the koftas.
- Cook on low heat till the gravy reaches the required consistency.
- Garnish with chopped coriander leaves and serve hot with rice.

Mithai

No Indian meal can be complete without a generous treat of sweets to the taste buds. The hospitable hosts never allow their guests to leave without the essential dessert followed by a paan *to aid digestion after the sumptuous meal. A rich variety of sweets is prepared in every Indian household. Popular amongst them are the various types of* laddoos, halwas *and syrup-based sweets.*

MOONG DAL HALWA *(A pulse-based sweet dish)*

Ingredients

- ¼ kg moong dal
- 1 cup ghee
- 1 cup sugar
- 1 litre milk
- 100 gms khoya
- ¼ tsp saffron dissolved in a little milk
- 2-3 green cardamoms, powdered
- Almonds for garnishing

Method

- Soak the dal overnight, wash and remove the husk.
- Grind coarsely in the mixie.
- Heat ghee in a deep pan. Reduce heat and add the ground moong dal. Fry on medium heat to a golden brown colour.
- Lower the flame and add milk. Cook till the milk thickens, add sugar and saffron.
- Fry till the ghee separates.
- Add the khoya and cardamom, mix well and remove from heat.
- Garnish with almonds. Serve hot or cold.

GAJAR HALWA *(Carrot halwa)*

Ingredients

- 8 cups of grated carrots
- 4 tbsp ghee
- 6 cups milk
- 2 cups sugar
- A few almonds and cashewnuts
- A few strands of saffron soaked in a little warm milk
- 3 green cardamoms, freshly ground

Method

❖ Fry the grated carrots in ghee. Add milk and cook till done.

❖ Add sugar, let simmer for a while till the sugar dissolves and the mixture thickens.

❖ Add the saffron and cardamom.

❖ Garnish with blanched and flaked almonds and fried cashewnuts.

❖ Serve hot or cold as desired.

KESAR PHIRNI
(Rice and milk-based sweet dish with a saffron flavour)

Ingredients

- 500 ml milk
- 50 gms sugar
- 75 gms rice flour
- A few strands of saffron
- 6-8 green cardamoms, powdered
- 25 gms pistachio
- 25 gms almonds

Method

❖ Boil the milk and reduce it to almost half the quantity.

❖ Add the rice flour, mix well to prevent lumps.

❖ Add the sugar and stir well till fully dissolved. Cook for a few minutes.

❖ Dissolve the saffron in warm milk and add it to the mixture.

❖ Pour the phirni into individual earthen bowls, garnish with chopped pistachios and almonds.

- Place it in the fridge to cool and set.
- The phirni should be yellowish in colour, grainy in texture and creamy in taste.
- Serve cold.

MOTICHOOR LADDOO
(Round sweet balls made of gramflour)

Ingredients

- 3 cups gramflour
- 4 cups sugar
- 2 cups water
- 3 tbsp rice flour
- Oil for frying

Method

- Mix gramflour and water to form a smooth, thick batter.
- Make a syrup by boiling the sugar and water.
- Heat oil in a kadai, hold a sieve over the hot oil. Gently tap the gramflour batter through the holes in the sieve into the oil. Remove the 'boondi' and place on paper napkins to absorb the excess oil. Repeat in batches.
- Quickly dip the 'boondis' in a bowlful of water. Lightly squeeze the 'boondis' and keep aside.
- Take 3 tbsp of the syrup and heat it in a pan. Add the 'boondis' and stir the mixture till it begins to leave the sides.
- Coat the hands with rice flour to avoid the stickiness and shape the warm mixture into lemon-sized balls.

KULFI *(Indian ice-cream)*

Ingredients

- 6 cups milk
- 1½ cups khoya
- 1 cup cream
- 8 tbsp cornflour
- 1¾ cups castor sugar
- A few drops of keora essence
- A few pieces of almonds and pistachios
- 4 green cardamoms, powdered

Method

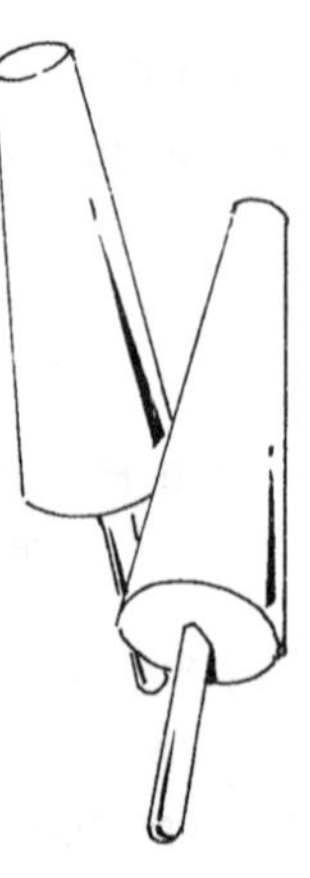

- ❖ Dissolve the cornflour in a little milk to obtain a thick paste.
- ❖ Boil the rest of the milk, add the dissolved cornflour and castor sugar and cook till the mixture thickens.
- ❖ Remove from fire, add the flavouring, cardamom powder and chopped nuts. Cool.
- ❖ Fill in kulfi moulds and place in the freezer for 6-8 hours or till it sets.
- ❖ Serve chilled.

JALEBI ***(Crisp coils of fried batter in syrup)***

Ingredients

- 2 cups maida
- ½ cup sugar
- 1¼ cups water
- ¼ cup curd
- 1 tsp rose water
- 1 pinch soda bicarb
- 1 pinch salt
- Oil for deep frying

Method

- ❖ Sift the flour and salt in a bowl.
- ❖ Combine the curd to give a batter of thick creamy consistency.
- ❖ Cover the bowl and let it stand for 6-7 hours to ferment.
- ❖ Boil the sugar in the water to make a syrup.
- ❖ Cool and add rose water.

- ❖ To the batter, add soda bicarb and mix well.
- ❖ Heat oil. Force the batter through a piping bag, forming spirals. Deep fry till golden brown.
- ❖ Immerse in the hot syrup and serve.

Chapter-2

The Southern Platter

Indian lands happen to be the epitome of generosity, be it in terms of culture, traditional values or in the production of spices: thus the cuisine.

It was, therefore, her pungent aromas which lured invaders and traders right from the time of Alexander to the Mughals, followed by the Dutch, French and the English. They all needed a tingling taste for their jaded palates and landed on our shores in search of spice in their lives. It was the Malabar coast, which saw all types of customers for its rich spices. Cardamom, pepper, cinnamon, cloves and nutmeg, you name it and it was grown there. Is it not a wonder that the South Indian flavour is one that consists all these aromas? The plentiful availability of coconuts, fish, root vegetables all along the coastline has influenced the culinary creations of this region.

Say South and one is reminded of *idlis, dosas* and the spicy-sour *sambar.* But there is much more to the Southern cuisine than *idlis* and *dosas*. Each vegetarian and non-vegetarian dish is a delicacy in its own right, especially with the blend of rich spices and coconut. Even though the basic tempering is the same (mustard seeds, whole red chillies, curry leaves, urad dal and chana dal with a pinch of asafoetida), the permutation and combination of other ingredients lend a different flavour to each dish. The *sambar* will taste different in an Iyengar household from Tamil Nadu, a Nair household from Kerala, a Shetty household from Andhra Pradesh and a Bhimmayya kitchen in Coorg.

Kerala, being blessed with an abundance of fish and coconut, the staple diet of the people is usually a preparation of fish accompanied with hot, steaming rice. In most vegetarian cooking, it is seen that the vegetables are usually parboiled and then tempered with mustard seeds, curry leaves and whole red chillies in coconut oil and finally laced with coconut milk. Banana chips and jackfruit chips are universally popular as snacks.

Hyderabadi cuisine has a definite Mughal influence. The *kababs* and *biryanis* are a hot favourite and chilli-hot, as well. The Nizams are believed to have been great patrons of good food. Hyderabadi cuisine took a definite shape under their patronage. Till date, the *kababs* and other meat dishes remain popular throughout the Southern region. Andhra food is known to be very spicy and hot. Traditional Andhra food is basically an off-shoot of the typical Southern cooking.

Vegetarian Delights

Coconut and tamarind form the base of basically all South Indian cooking. Rice forms the staple diet of the people which is served steaming hot along with dals, usually sambar, ericheri, *dry vegetable preparations, fried* pappads, chutneys, *pickles and* dal *powders. Tempering with mustard seeds, curry leaves,* urad dal *and* chana dal *is given to basically all preparations, irrespective of the cultural and geographical divisions among the four states comprising the south of India.*

AVIAL

(A mixed vegetable preparation in curd base from Kerala)

Ingredients

- 2 brinjals
- 2 raw bananas
- 2 potatoes
- 2 carrots
- 100 gms French beans
- 100 gms cluster beans
- 2 large pieces pumpkin
- 3 drumsticks
- Half a coconut
- 2 cups sour curd
- 5 green chillies
- ½ tbsp turmeric powder
- ½ tbsp cumin seeds
- Salt to taste

For Tempering

- Coconut oil
- A few sprigs curry leaves
- 5 gms mustard seeds

Method

- Wash and clean vegetables and cut into 2" long pieces and parboil with turmeric powder and a pinch of salt.
- Grate coconut and grind it with green chillies and cumin seeds to a smooth paste.
- Place cooked vegetables in a vessel. Add ground ingredients, salt to taste and curd. Simmer on low fire for a few minutes. Add coconut oil, temper with curry leaves and mustard and remove from fire. Serve hot with rice.

PARUPPU USILI *(A cluster bean and lentil dish)*

Ingredients

- ¼ kg cluster beans
- ½ cup arhar dal
- 4 red chillies
- 1 tsp mustard seeds
- A small pinch of asafoetida
- Oil for frying
- Salt to taste

Method

- Soak dal in water for an hour. Grind (without water) it to a coarse paste with red chillies, asafoetida and salt to taste.
- Chop cluster beans. Mix the beans with the dal paste and cook till done.
- Heat oil in a frying pan and add mustard seeds. When they crackle, add the cooked cluster beans and fry well.
- Fry on low fire till the mixture becomes dry. Serve hot.

MIXED VEGETABLE STEW
(Mixed vegetables cooked in coconut milk)

Ingredients

- ½ kg mixed vegetables (French beans, carrots, green peas and potatoes)
- 2 cups grated coconut
- 1 cup sliced onion
- 6 green chillies, slit
- 1 dessertspoon garlic
- 1" piece of ginger
- 1" piece of cinnamon
- 5 cloves
- 1 tsp peppercorns
- 1 tbsp ghee
- 2 sprigs curry leaves
- Salt to taste

Method

- Grind ginger and garlic to paste.
- Powder peppercorns, cloves and cinnamon. In a pan, heat oil, sauté onions, green chillies, ginger and garlic till lightly brown.

- Add the curry leaves, vegetables and the powdered masala. Sauté again.
- Extract one cup thick coconut milk and two cups thin coconut milk.
- Add the thin coconut milk to the vegetables and cook till done. Add salt.
- Add the thick coconut milk, stir well and remove from heat.
- Serve hot with appams.

LADYFINGERS IN CURD

Ingredients

- 200 gms lady fingers
- 500 gms curd
- 2 onions
- 2 green chillies, slit lengthwise
- 2 sprigs curry leaves
- 50 ml oil
- 1 tbsp coconut oil
- 4 whole red chillies
- ½ tbsp turmeric powder
- ½ tbsp mustard seeds
- ¼ tbsp fenugreek seeds
- Salt to taste

Method

- Cut ladyfingers into ½" long pieces. Whip curd with turmeric powder and keep aside.
- Heat oil in a pan, season it with mustard seeds, fenugreek seeds, red chillies and curry leaves.
- When the mustard seeds crackle, add sliced onions and slit green chillies. Sauté well.
- Add ladyfingers and fry well. Finally add the whipped curd, salt to taste and simmer on low heat.
- Serve hot, laced with coconut oil.

TOMATO PANCHAMRITA
(A sweet and sour tomato preparation)

Ingredients

- 500 gms ripe tomatoes
- A handful of roasted groundnuts, crushed
- A small ball of jaggery
- 4-5 green chillies
- ½ tsp mustard seeds
- ¼ tsp turmeric powder
- A pinch of asafoetida
- 1 tbsp ghee
- A pinch of salt

Method

- ❖ Wash and cut each tomato into 8 pieces. Slice the chillies lengthwise.
- ❖ Heat ghee and prepare a seasoning with mustard seeds, turmeric powder and asafoetida.
- ❖ Add chillies and fry for some time. Put in the tomato pieces, salt and jaggery and allow to steam cook.
- ❖ Lastly add the crushed groundnuts. Mix well and remove the vessel from heat.
- ❖ This dish should be slightly sweet.

TOMATO-CHILLI RASAM
(A hot and spicy Indian soup)

Ingredients

- 300 gms tomatoes, chopped fine
- 4 tbsp arhar dal
- 20 gms tamarind
- 2 sprigs curry leaves
- A small bunch coriander leaves, chopped
- 2 whole red chillies
- ¼ tsp turmeric powder
- A pinch asafoetida
- 1 tsp rasam powder
- ¼ tsp peppercorns, crushed
- 2 tbsp ghee
- ¼ tsp mustard seeds
- Salt to taste

Method

- ❖ Boil the arhar dal with turmeric powder and half a litre water till cooked.

- Strain the dal, reserve the water for later use. Mash the dal lightly.
- Soak tamarind in warm water, extract pulp and keep aside.
- Bring one cup water to a boil. Add chopped tomatoes, tamarind pulp, asafoetida, chopped coriander leaves, curry leaves and rasam powder.
- Cook over low heat for 10-15 minutes. Add the reserved dal water, and simmer. Sprinkle crushed peppercorns.
- Heat ghee. Temper with mustard seeds and red chillies. Pour over the rasam.
- Serve hot, garnished with coriander leaves.

MALABAR APPAMS *(Rice flour pancakes)*

Ingredients

- 3 cups raw rice flour
- 1 large coconut, grated
- 1 cup coconut milk, for kneading
- ½ cup lukewarm water
- 2 tbsp sugar
- 1 tbsp dry yeast
- 1 dessertspoon semolina
- ½ tsp salt

Method

- Mix sugar and yeast and cover with a little warm water. Keep aside for 10-15 minutes until froth appears on the surface and starts cracking.
- Mix well until the sugar and yeast granules are dissolved. Keep aside.
- Cook the semolina with ½ cup water to make a porridge. Sieve the rice flour in a bowl, pour the semolina porridge into it and mix well.
- Add the yeast ferment and the coconut milk. Knead well for at least 10 minutes, folding it several times, till a soft dough is obtained.
- Keep the dough aside to ferment for 5-6 hours (smearing a little coconut milk will make the dough softer).

- ❖ Extract about three cups coconut milk, add it to the fermented dough and make a thin batter without any lumps.
- ❖ Add sugar according to taste and allow the batter to ferment for another 1½ to two hours. Add salt and mix well.
- ❖ Heat a cast iron kadai. Rub with oil. Pour three to four tbsp of the batter into the kadai.
- ❖ Spread the batter by rotating the kadai so that about 2½" of kadai is thinly coated and the remaining batter collects at the centre. Care should be taken to rotate the kadai only once.
- ❖ Cover with a tight fitting lid with a handle (preferably metallic). Lower the heat and cook for 3-4 minutes.
- ❖ When appams are ready, their edges resemble crisp lace and the centre is soft and well risen. Best when served hot with mutton stew.

BEANS THORAN

(A French bean preparation with coconut)

Ingredients

- 450 gms French beans
- 50 gms onions
- 4-5 green chillies
- 1 tsp mustard seeds
- 30 ml oil
- 50 gms coconut, grated
- 1 sprig curry leaves
- Salt to taste

Method

- ❖ Wash, string and slice beans into small pieces.
- ❖ Chop onions and green chillies.
- ❖ Heat oil, add mustard seeds. When mustard seeds crackle, add chopped onion, green chillies and curry leaves. Sauté.
- ❖ Add sliced beans, salt and enough water to cook beans. Cook until water evaporates.
- ❖ Add grated coconut. Cook a little longer, stir well and remove from fire. Serve hot.

KHOLAMBA

(A brinjal and gram preparation in a sour base)

Ingredients

- 3-4 brinjals, cut into big pieces
- ½ cup red gram dal
- 2-3 red chillies, chopped
- 1 tbsp tamarind pulp
- 2 tbsp kholamba powder
- ½ tsp mustard seeds
- A few curry leaves
- A pinch of asafoetida
- 1 tbsp oil
- Salt to taste

FOR KHOLAMBA MASALA

- 200 gms coriander seeds
- 25 gms red chillies
- 5 gms mustard seeds
- 5 gms cumin seeds
- 1 tsp black gram dal
- 1 tsp Bengal gram dal
- 1 tsp fenugreek seeds
- ½ tsp turmeric powder
- ½ tsp black peppercorns
- ½ tsp asafoetida
- 2 tbsp curry leaves
- Oil for frying

Method

- ❖ To prepare the kholamba masala, fry the ingredients separately on low flame until they are light brown in colour. Pound them together and sieve. Blend the masala well and store in an airtight jar.
- ❖ Wash and cook the dal. Cook the brinjals separately with enough water till soft. Add salt, tamarind pulp and one teaspoon of kholamba powder to the dal. Stir well and add enough water and bring to a boil.
- ❖ Heat oil and prepare the seasoning with mustard seeds, red chillies, curry leaves and asafoetida. Add the seasoning to the dal.
- ❖ Serve hot with rice.

SAMBAR

(Lentil and mixed vegetables with a tangy taste)

Ingredients

- 2 cups arhar dal
- 1 cup mixed vegetables (brinjals, French beans, etc.)
- 2 onions (chopped)
- 2 tbsp coconut
- 2 tbsp coriander seeds
- 1 large pinch each of fenugreek seeds, asafoetida and turmeric
- 2 tbsp oil
- 1 tsp mustard seeds
- 4 sprigs curry leaves
- 2 tbsp coriander leaves (chopped)
- A lemon-sized ball of tamarind
- Salt to taste

Method

- ❖ Chop the vegetables into pieces. Clean and wash the dal.
- ❖ Cook the dal till soft. Beat well till it blends.
- ❖ Add vegetables and onions, and boil. Keep aside.
- ❖ Roast coriander seeds, fenugreek seeds and asafoetida in half the oil. Grind this masala with coconut and tamarind to a smooth paste. Add to the dal.
- ❖ Add turmeric, salt and a little water to get the right consistency of the dal. Boil for a minute.
- ❖ Heat oil and add mustard seeds, curry leaves. When the mustard seeds splutter, add the tempering to the dal.
- ❖ Serve hot with idli, dosa or rice.

RAW BANANA AND CHAVLI SUBJI

Ingredients

- 300 gms raw bananas
- 150 gms long beans (chavli)
- 6 whole red chillies, deseeded and chopped
- 2 sprigs curry leaves
- 1 tsp mustard seeds
- 2 tsp coriander powder
- 2 tsp chilli powder
- ½ tsp turmeric powder
- 3 tbsp coconut oil
- Salt to taste

Method

- ❖ Apply a little oil on the palms. Carefully remove the green outer layer of the raw bananas (not the entire peel), dice them.
- ❖ Put the diced bananas in a pan full of salted water and boil till cooked.
- ❖ String the beans and cut them into 1½" long pieces. Blanch in salted, boiling water for two to three minutes. Drain.
- ❖ Heat oil in a kadai and season with mustard seeds. When they crackle, add red chillies and curry leaves.
- ❖ Mix coriander powder, chilli powder and turmeric powder in about 3 tablespoon water and add to the pan. Stir till the moisture evaporates.
- ❖ Add the bananas and the beans and stir fry for three to four minutes.
- ❖ Remove from heat and serve hot with Malabar parathas.

SPINACH-POTATO FRY

Ingredients

- 800 gms red spinach
- 200 gms potatoes, peeled and diced
- 90 gms coconut, grated
- Salt to taste

For Tempering

- 2 tbsp coconut oil
- 1 tsp mustard seeds
- 1 tsp urad dal, washed and dried
- 1 onion, sliced
- 2 sprigs curry leaves
- 1" piece of ginger, julienned
- 6 green chillies, julienned

Method

- ❖ Parboil the potatoes with salt, drain and keep aside.
- ❖ Heat oil in a kadai. Add mustard seeds. When they splutter, add urad dal and fry till golden brown. Add onions and fry till translucent. Add ginger, green chillies and curry leaves and fry well.

- Add the spinach and fry till almost dry. Then put the potatoes and cook till done and the moisture evaporates.
- Add grated coconut and toss for a minute.
- Remove from heat and serve hot as an accompaniment with rice.

RAW BANANA THORAN
(Raw bananas in a coconut base)

Ingredients

- 500 gms raw bananas
- ½ coconut, grated
- 10 gms green chillies
- ½ tsp turmeric powder
- 1 clove of garlic
- 1 onion
- 2 sprigs curry leaves
- Salt to taste

To Temper

- 15 ml coconut oil
- 2 onions

Method

- Peel and cut bananas into cubes. Wash well.
- Add just enough water to cook.
- Add salt. Grind together green chillies, turmeric powder, coconut, garlic and onion.
- Add the ground masala to the cooked banana. Cook for a few minutes. Mix well.
- Add curry leaves and remove from fire.
- Heat oil in a frying pan. Add sliced onions and fry till brown. Add the banana mixture.
- Stir well for 2-3 minutes.
- Serve hot.

STUFFED PADAVAL
(Snake gourd stuffed with potatoes)

Ingredients

- 450 gms snake gourd
- 225 gms potatoes
- 50 gms onions
- 10 gms green chillies
- 30 gms gramflour
- ½ lime
- A small piece of ginger
- A pinch of mustard seeds
- A pinch of turmeric powder
- 600 ml water
- 30 gms oil
- Salt to taste

Method

- Wash and cut each snake gourd into half. Steam the snake gourd until half cooked.
- Cut into 2" pieces and remove the seeds. Apply salt and set aside.
- Boil potatoes, peel and dice.
- Finely chop onions, green chillies and ginger.
- Heat a little oil, add mustard seeds. When they crackle, add chillies, onion, ginger, turmeric powder, potatoes and salt. Mix well.
- Add lime juice to the potato mixture and blend well. Remove from the fire.
- Stuff the snake gourd with the potato mixture.
- Prepare a batter with gramflour, salt and water.
- Dip the stuffed gourd in the batter and deep fry in hot oil.
- Serve hot with tamarind chutney or ketchup.

CHEMBU CURRY *(Colocasia with coconut)*

Ingredients

- 500 gms arvi
- 5 gms kokum
- ½ coconut, grated
- 10 gms green chillies
- 1 onion
- 3 cloves of garlic
- 2 sprigs curry leaves
- 1 tsp turmeric powder
- 30 ml coconut oil
- Salt to taste

Method

- ❖ Peel arvi, wash well. Put into cold water and bring to a boil. Drain.
- ❖ Add salt, washed kokum and just enough water to cook the arvi.
- ❖ Grind together the coconut, green chillies, turmeric powder, garlic and onions into a fine paste.
- ❖ When the arvi is tender and the moisture has evaporated, add the ground mixture.
- ❖ Mix well and stir over low fire for about 2 minutes.
- ❖ Add curry leaves and fresh coconut oil. Remove from fire. Serve hot.

RAW JACKFRUIT CURRY

Ingredients

- 1 medium raw jackfruit
- 1 coconut, grated
- 10-15 gms green chillies
- 1 onion
- 1 tsp turmeric powder
- ½ tsp cumin seeds
- A few sprigs of curry leaves
- Salt to taste

To Temper

- 30 ml coconut oil
- 1 onion
- 1 tsp mustard seeds

Method

- ❖ Cut the jackfruit into quarters. Cut off the white pith on top.
- ❖ Using oiled hands, remove seeds and slice into thin long pieces.
- ❖ In a pan, put the jackfruit pieces, add salt and enough water to cook. Cover the pan and boil the jackfruit.
- ❖ Grind together cumin seeds, green chillies, turmeric powder, coconut and onion.
- ❖ Mix the ground masala with the cooked jackfruit, blend well and cook for about 3-4 minutes. Add the curry leaves.

- Heat oil, add mustard seeds and when they splutter, add sliced onions and fry till brown.
- Add the jackfruit mixture and cook for 2-3 minutes. Remove from fire.
- Serve hot.

MOR KOZHAMBU

(White pumpkin cooked with sour curd)

Ingredients

- 500 gms white pumpkin or sooran
- 500 gms sour curd
- 1 coconut
- 4-5 green chillies
- 1" piece ginger
- 1 tbsp coriander powder
- 1 tsp chilli powder
- 100 gms chana dal, soaked
- ½ tbsp cumin seeds
- Salt to taste

Method

- Chop the pumpkin into large pieces and pressure cook till one whistle.
- Grate the coconut and grind it with coriander powder, ginger and red chillies to make a fine paste.
- Grind the chana dal separately.
- Fry the pumpkin and add the ground chana dal and cook till done.
- Add the ground masala, stir and remove from fire.
- Serve hot.

BAGARA BAINGAN

(A Hyderabadi speciality—Spicy and sour brinjal preparation cooked with coconut)

Ingredients

- 450 gms brinjals
- 115 gms coconut
- 4 large onions
- 115 gms tamarind
- 4-6 cloves garlic
- 5-6 red chillies
- 1 tbsp jaggery
- 2-3 green chillies
- 3 tsp coriander seeds
- 1 tbsp gingelly seeds
- ¼ tsp mustard seeds
- ½ tsp turmeric powder
- 1 sprig curry leaves
- Oil for cooking
- Salt to taste

Method

- Wash the brinjals without breaking the stem. Cut them lengthwise in quarters.
- Heat the oil and fry brinjals until the skin gets a brownish colour. Remove and keep aside.
- In the same oil, fry the coriander seeds, chillies and onions. Grind them with coconut and garlic.
- Roast gingelly seeds separately and powder.
- Soak the tamarind and extract the pulp. Add this pulp to the ground masalas.
- Heat some oil and fry the masala till oil floats on top. Add the brinjals and gingelly powder. Cover and cook till the gravy thickens.
- When the gravy is quite thick, remove from fire.
- In another pan, heat a little oil, add mustard seeds and curry leaves. When the mustard seeds crackle, pour over the curry. Mix well and serve hot.

ERICHERI *(Yam and raw banana preparation)*

Ingredients

- 250 gms yam
- 2 raw bananas
- 1 coconut
- 1 tsp peppercorns
- 1 tsp mustard seeds
- 1 tsp raw rice
- ½ tsp turmeric powder
- Coconut oil for tempering
- Salt to taste

Method

- ❖ Peel yam and raw bananas and slice into 1" pieces.
- ❖ Cook the pieces in 1 cup water with turmeric powder.
- ❖ Grind peppercorns to a smooth paste and add to the cooked yam and bananas. Cook on slow fire for a few minutes.
- ❖ Grind coconut to a coarse paste. Remove half of the ground coconut and keep aside. To the remaining coconut, add raw rice and grind to a smooth paste.
- ❖ Heat a little oil and fry the coarsely ground coconut.
- ❖ Add the yam, bananas, coconut paste and salt.
- ❖ Allow to cook till done.
- ❖ Heat a little coconut oil, add the mustard seeds. When they crackle, add the curry leaves and pour over the ericheri. Serve hot.

YOGIRATHNA *(Mixed vegetable curry)*

Ingredients

- 3 potatoes
- ½ cup green peas, shelled
- A small piece of ash gourd
- 1 cucumber
- 1 vegetable marrow
- 1 carrot
- A small piece of cauliflower
- 2 tomatoes
- 2 onions
- A small piece of ginger
- 6 green chillies
- 1 coconut
- 1 tsp coriander seeds
- 1 tsp poppy seeds
- 1 tsp mustard seeds
- 1 tsp cumin seeds
- A few sprigs curry leaves
- A pinch of asafoetida
- Oil for frying
- Salt to taste

Method

- ❖ Wash and peel potatoes, marrow, carrot, cucumber and ash gourd. Cut into cubes.
- ❖ Chop tomatoes and onions and cauliflower into florets and slit the green chillies. Grate coconut and extract the milk.
- ❖ Grind poppy seeds, coriander seeds and ginger to a smooth paste.
- ❖ Cook with green chillies, coconut milk and the ground masala with 1½ cups of water. Continue to simmer on low flame.
- ❖ Heat oil in a pan, add mustard, cumin seeds, curry leaves and asafoetida. As soon as the mustard crackles, remove from fire and temper the curry with this seasoning. Serve hot.

TAMARIND RICE

(Rice flavoured with spices in tamarind pulp)

Ingredients

- 400 gms rice
- 50 gms tamarind
- 20 gms red chillies
- 50 gms urad dal
- 50 gms chana dal
- 150 ml mustard oil
- 1 tsp asafoetida
- A pinch mustard seeds
- 1 green chilli
- A small piece ginger, julienned
- A few peppercorns
- A pinch turmeric powder
- A few sprigs curry leaves, chopped
- 200 ml water, for soaking tamarind
- 50 gms groundnuts
- Salt to taste

Method

- ❖ Cook the rice with salt till done and leave to cool.
- ❖ Soak tamarind in 200 ml water and extract pulp.
- ❖ Roast urad dal, chana dal and red chillies separately and grind to a coarse powder.

- Heat oil in a pan, add asafoetida, mustard seeds, peppercorns, turmeric powder, green chilli, ginger and curry leaves. When mustard seeds crackle, add tamarind pulp, powdered masala and salt to taste.
- Cook till all the water evaporates and the mixture thickens. Add this tamarind masala to the rice and mix well till the rice is well coated. Remove from fire and serve hot, garnished with fried groundnuts.

VEGETABLE UPMA

(A breakfast and snack item made of semolina and vegetables)

Ingredients

- 1 cup semolina
- 2 tomatoes, chopped
- 1 onion
- ½ cup shelled green peas
- ¼ cup cauliflower florets
- ¼ cup diced carrot
- 2 green chillies, chopped
- ¼ tsp mustard seeds
- ¼ tsp urad dal
- ¼ tsp chana dal
- A few curry leaves
- 1 tbsp oil
- 2 cups water
- Grated coconut for garnishing
- Salt to taste

Method

- Roast the semolina till it changes colour. Keep aside to cool.
- Parboil the cauliflower, carrot and peas.
- Heat the oil, add the mustard seeds, chana dal and urad dal. When the dals turn brown, add the curry leaves.
- Fry the onions till they are transparent. Add the tomatoes and cook till the oil floats on top.
- Add the parboiled vegetables, salt and water.
- When the water boils, slowly add the roasted semolina, while stirring constantly.
- Garnish with grated coconut and serve hot.

LEMON RICE *(Lemon flavoured rice)*

Ingredients

- 250 gms rice
- Juice of 2 lemons
- ½ tsp mustard seeds
- 1 tsp urad dal
- 1 tsp chana dal
- 4 red chillies, chopped
- 100 gms groundnuts, fried
- 2 sprigs curry leaves
- 2 green chillies
- 1" piece of ginger, julienned
- ½ tsp turmeric powder
- ¼ tsp asafoetida
- 50 gms coriander leaves, chopped
- 50 ml oil
- Salt to taste

Method

- Boil rice till half done and keep aside to cool.
- Heat oil and season with mustard seeds, urad dal, chana dal, red chillies and curry leaves.
- Add chopped ginger and stir lightly. Add green chillies and toss. Add turmeric powder, asafoetida and salt.
- Toss the cooked rice in this mixture. Sprinkle lemon juice and cook for a few more minutes.
- Serve hot, garnished with fried groundnuts and chopped coriander leaves.

COCONUT RICE

Ingredients

- 250 gms rice
- 1 coconut, grated
- 2 onions, chopped
- 6 red chillies, chopped
- 2 green chillies, slit lengthwise
- ½ tsp mustard seeds
- 50 gms coriander leaves, chopped
- 1 tsp urad dal
- 2 sprigs curry leaves
- 50 ml oil
- Salt to taste

Method

- Boil the rice till half done. Cool and keep aside.
- Heat oil and temper with mustard seeds, urad dal, red chillies and curry leaves.

- When the mustard seeds crackle, add chopped onions and green chillies. Fry till the onions are brown.
- Add grated coconut, reserving a little for garnishing. Sauté without letting the mixture turn brown.
- Add the cooked rice, salt, coriander leaves tossing continuously. Remove from fire.
- Garnish with grated coconut and serve hot.

BISI BELE BHATH

(A Karnataka special rice with mixed vegetables and pulses)

Ingredients

- 250 gms rice
- 75 gms arhar dal
- 2 brinjals
- 2 carrots
- 3 drumsticks
- A handful of Madras onions
- A small piece of vegetable marrow
- Lemon-sized ball of tamarind
- 12 red chillies
- 4 green chillies
- 1 tsp fenugreek seeds
- 1 tbsp coriander seeds
- 2 tsp mustard seeds
- 1 tsp poppy seeds
- ½ tbsp aniseed
- 4 cloves
- 4 cardamoms
- A small piece of cinnamon
- 25 gms cashewnuts
- ½ coconut, grated
- A pinch of asafoetida
- 2 sprigs of curry leaves
- 50 gms coriander leaves
- Ghee for frying
- Salt to taste

Method

- Peel the Madras onions and the vegetables. Cut the vegetables into 1" pieces.
- Wash the rice and dal thoroughly.
- Cook the rice and dal with a pinch of turmeric powder and chopped vegetables.
- Heat a little oil in a frying pan. Add red chillies, fenugreek seeds, coriander seeds and grated coconut. Fry until the fenugreek seeds turn golden brown in colour.
- Powder and keep aside.

- Heat a little oil and fry the poppy seeds, cloves, cinnamon, cardamom and aniseed. Powder and keep aside.
- Soak tamarind in a little water and extract the pulp.
- Heat a little oil, add the remaining chillies, mustard, curry leaves and green chillies. When the mustard crackles, add to the rice and mix well.
- Add tamarind pulp and salt and mix thoroughly.
- Heat a little ghee and fry the cashewnuts until golden brown in colour. Add to the rice along with the powdered ingredients.
- Mix well. Remove from fire. Add a dash of ghee just before serving.

CURD RICE

Ingredients

- 250 gms boiled rice
- 2 cups fresh curd
- ½ tsp mustard seeds
- 50 gms broken cashewnuts
- 2 whole red chillies
- 2 green chillies, chopped
- A small piece of ginger
- 2 sprigs of curry leaves
- A few coriander leaves
- Salt to taste
- 1 tbsp oil

Method

- Wash and cook the rice. Keep aside.
- When cool, mix the curd thoroughly with the rice.
- Heat the oil and add the mustard seeds, red chillies and curry leaves.
- When the mustard seeds crackle, add the green chillies, ginger, and salt.
- Pour over the cooked rice.
- Garnish with cashewnuts and coriander leaves. Serve cold.

In the South, it is usually the fish that takes an upper hand in the menu. Like in the other curries, coconut and chillies take pride of place in the list of ingredients. Unlike the North, the meat is not marinated and fried for long.

FRIED MUTTON WITH COCONUT

Ingredients

- 500 gm boneless mutton, cubed
- 2 onions, sliced
- 2 green chillies, slit lengthwise
- 1 tomato, chopped
- 1 tsp ginger-garlic paste
- 1 tsp red chilli paste
- 2 sprigs curry leaves
- 1 tbsp coriander powder
- ½ tsp fennel seeds, powdered
- 3" piece of dried coconut, sliced
- A few coriander leaves
- 180 ml oil
- Salt to taste

Method

- Parboil the mutton and keep aside.
- Heat oil and fry the sliced onions till golden brown. Add the green chillies, ginger-garlic paste and stir fry. Stir in the red chilli paste, coriander powder and salt.
- Add the curry leaves and fry till oil floats on top.
- Add the chopped tomatoes and cook till the masala is dry.
- Add the mutton and slices of dry coconut in the masala and cook till the mutton is soft and tender.
- Sprinkle fennel powder and garnish with coriander leaves. Serve hot.

MUTTON STEW *(Mutton cooked in coconut milk)*

Ingredients

- ½ kg mutton pieces
- 1 coconut, grated
- 4 chopped onions
- ½ cup coconut slices
- 4-5 cloves
- 2" piece of ginger, finely chopped
- 4-5 green chillies, finely chopped
- 1½" piece cinnamon
- ¼ cup peppercorns
- ½ cup coconut oil
- Salt to taste

Method

- Grind the coconut and take the first and second extract of milk.
- Heat oil in a pan and fry green chillies, ginger, peppercorns, cloves and cinnamon. Add mutton and fry for a few minutes.
- Add thin coconut milk along with salt. Pressure cook till done. Finally stir in the thick coconut milk.
- To season, heat a little oil, fry the onion slices and coconut slices till light brown.
- Add to the stew. Remove from fire. Serve hot with appams.

FRIED PRAWNS

Ingredients

- 200 gms prawns
- Juice of 1 lemon
- 1 tsp red chilli paste
- 1 tsp ginger-garlic paste
- ½ tsp turmeric powder
- 1 tbsp cumin powder
- Oil for frying
- Salt to taste

Method

- Shell, devein and clean the prawns.
- Mix all the remaining ingredients, except oil, and apply it on the prawns. Keep aside for half an hour to marinate.

- Heat oil in a shallow pan and fry the prawns. Cook for three minutes, remove and drain.
- Serve hot, garnished with rings of onions and fried curry leaves.

PRAWN PULAO

Ingredients

- 300 gms basmati rice
- 1 tbsp lemon juice
- 5 onions
- 175 gms ghee
- Salt to taste

For The Pouch

- 5 green cardamoms
- 1" piece cinnamon
- 2 cloves
- 2 bay leaves

For The Prawns

- 400 gms prawns
- 12 cloves of garlic, sliced
- 1" piece ginger, julienned
- 4 green chillies, slit, deseeded
- 1 tsp coriander powder
- ½ tsp chilli powder
- ¼ tsp turmeric powder
- 2 sprigs curry leaves
- 2 tsp coconut oil
- Salt to taste

Method

- Clean and wash the rice. Soak it for 45 minutes. Keep aside.
- Shell, devein and clean the prawns.
- Pound the garam masala and tie in a piece of clean muslin cloth.
- In a large pan, take 1½ litres of water, add salt and the pouch and bring to a boil.
- Add the rice when the water is boiling. Stir occasionally until the rice is cooked. Add the lemon juice and mix well. Drain the water and discard the pouch of garam masala.
- Heat oil. Temper with ginger, garlic, curry leaves and green chillies. Stir over medium heat until the garlic is golden.

- ❖ Mix coriander powder, chilli powder and turmeric powder in 2 tablespoon of water to form a smooth paste. Add this to the tempering and cook till the moisture evaporates.
- ❖ Add the prawns and salt. Sauté for 3 minutes. Remove from heat and keep aside.
- ❖ Heat ghee in a pan. Add onions and fry till golden. Add the prawns, stir till the moisture has evaporated.
- ❖ Add the rice and mix gently. Cook for 2-3 minutes.
- ❖ Serve hot.

COORG FRIED CHICKEN

Ingredients

- 16 pieces chicken drumsticks
- 150 gms onions
- 25 gms garlic
- 75 ml oil
- 15 ml vinegar
- 5 gms cinnamon
- 5 gms cloves
- 1 tsp red chilli powder
- 5 gms Coorg garam masala
- Salt to taste

For The Coorg Garam Masala

- 20 gms coriander seeds
- 10 gms black peppercorns
- 5 gms jeera
- 5 gms mustard seeds

Method

- ❖ Roast the Coorg garam masala till brown and powder it. Marinate the chicken drumsticks with this masala and salt, for 30 minutes.
- ❖ Heat oil in a pan, add chopped garlic and onions. Sauté till brown.
- ❖ Add the rest of the garam masala and red chilli powder.
- ❖ Add the chicken drumsticks and cook it in its own juices.
- ❖ When it is half done, add the vinegar. Cook till it dries. Serve hot garnished with lemon wedges and onion rings.

MEEN MOILEE ***(Fish curry in coconut milk)***

Ingredients

- 6 pomfrets
- 3 large onions, sliced
- 1" piece of ginger, julienned
- 6 green chillies, deseeded and julienned
- 8 cloves garlic, chopped fine
- 3 large tomatoes, sliced
- 1 tbsp lemon juice
- ½ tsp turmeric powder
- 1 tsp mustard seeds
- 1 coconut, grated
- 2 sprigs curry leaves
- 2 tbsp coconut oil
- Salt to taste

Method

- Cut the pomfrets into fillets.
- Grind the coconut and extract half cup of thick milk, add some water and obtain half a cup of second extract and half a cup of third extract.
- Heat oil in a pan and add mustard seeds. Stir till they begin to splutter. Add garlic and ginger and stir for a minute. Add green chillies and onions and fry till onions turn glossy.
- Add turmeric powder and mix well. Slip the fillets and the third extract of the coconut milk. Bring it to a boil. Lower the heat and simmer for 3 minutes, turning the fillets carefully.
- Add salt, curry leaves, tomatoes and the second extract. Cover and simmer for another 3 minutes. Remove the pan from heat and gently stir in the first extract of coconut milk.
- Return the pan to heat and bring to a boil over low heat. Sprinkle lemon juice and mix carefully.
- Serve hot with rice.

FISH MAPPAS *(Fish in coconut gravy)*

Ingredients

- 750 gms fish, cut into pieces
- 2 cups grated coconut
- 1 cup onion, sliced
- 10 green chillies
- 1 tsp garlic, sliced
- ½ tsp ginger, sliced
- 1½ tsp vinegar
- ½ tsp fenugreek seeds
- ½ tsp mustard seeds
- A few curry leaves
- 2 tbsp oil
- Salt to taste

Grind Together

- 7 red chillies
- 2 tsp coriander seeds
- 1 tsp peppercorns
- 1 tsp turmeric powder
- 1 tsp garlic paste
- 1 onion

Method

- ❖ Grind the coconut and extract 1 cup thick coconut milk. Add a little water and extract 3 cups of thin coconut milk.
- ❖ Split green chillies. Heat oil and season it with fenugreek seeds, mustard seeds and curry leaves.
- ❖ Add the ground masala paste and fry well. Add the sliced ginger, green chillies, onion and garlic. Fry till they turn brown in colour.
- ❖ Add the thin coconut milk, salt and vinegar. Bring it to a boil. Add the fish pieces and let the curry simmer over low fire.
- ❖ When the fish is cooked and the gravy is thick enough, stir in the thick coconut milk.
- ❖ Bring it to a boil and remove from fire.
- ❖ Serve hot with rice.

ALLEPEY FISH *(Sour fish curry)*

Ingredients

- 500 gms fish cubes, (½ inch)
- 150 gms onions, sliced
- 25 gms root ginger, peeled and shredded

- 4 green chillies, slit
- 15 curry leaves
- 50 ml coconut oil
- 300 gms raw mangoes, peeled and finely diced
- 350 ml coconut cream
- 150 ml coconut milk
- ½ tsp chilli powder
- ½ tsp turmeric powder
- Salt to taste

Method

- ❖ Heat oil in a kadai, add the sliced onions, slit green chillies, curry leaves and ginger. Sauté till onions are transparent.
- ❖ Add the chilli and turmeric powders and sauté for 2-3 minutes.
- ❖ Add the fish and salt. Cook for about 5 minutes.
- ❖ Add the raw mangoes and simmer for a few more minutes until the fish flakes easily.
- ❖ Stir in thick coconut milk. Remove from fire.
- ❖ Just before serving, pour in the coconut cream and serve hot.

CHICKEN IN COCONUT

Ingredients

- 1 chicken, cut into medium sized pieces
- 2 coconuts, grated
- 250 gms onions
- 6 green chillies, slit lengthwise
- 1" piece of ginger, ground to paste
- 2 sprigs curry leaves
- 100 ml refined oil
- 50 ml coconut oil
- 25 gms coriander seeds
- 8 red chillies
- 10 gms fennel seeds
- ½ tsp turmeric powder
- ½ tsp mustard seeds
- Salt to taste

Method

- ❖ Roast the coriander seeds, red chillies and fennel seeds and grind to a smooth paste along with onions.
- ❖ Mix turmeric powder, slit green chillies, ginger paste and salt. Marinate the chicken pieces in this mixture, for half an hour.

- Heat the oils (refined and coconut) in a kadai and fry the ground masala paste till the oil floats on top.
- Add the chicken pieces, sauté for a few minutes, sprinkle ½ cup water, cover and cook on medium heat until done.
- Grind the coconut, extract the milk, add to the curry.
- Heat oil in a pan, add mustard seeds, curry leaves and 2 whole red chillies. Pour over curry. Serve hot.

NAWABI PULAO

(A blend of mutton, chicken and egg with rice)

Ingredients

- ½ chicken
- ¼ kg mutton
- ½ kg rice
- 1 cup curd, well beaten
- 1 cup milk
- 3 onions
- 2 eggs
- ½ cup green peas, shelled
- 1 pod garlic
- 1 big piece of ginger
- 1 tsp rose water
- Ghee or oil for frying
- Salt to taste

Method

- Clean and wash rice and soak it in water for 15 minutes.
- Cook the rice till half done. Keep aside.
- Clean and cut the mutton into cubes. Joint the chicken. Boil the eggs and keep aside.
- Boil green peas with salt and keep aside.
- Slice the onions. Grind ginger and garlic to a paste.
- Heat ghee in a frying pan, add onions, ginger-garlic paste and fry well.
- Add the jointed chicken and fry. Add 3 cups water and salt to taste and cook on slow fire till the meat is tender and only $^{1}/_{3rd}$ of the gravy is left.
- Add some more ghee and the well beaten curd. Cook on a slow fire until the curd gets absorbed.

- Add 1 teaspoon of rose water after the meat has cooled.
- Take a heavy bottomed pan and arrange alternate layers of rice and cooked meat taking care that the first and last layers are that of rice.
- Place in an oven and cook for about 15-20 minutes on low heat.
- Garnish with fried onions, quartered boiled eggs and boiled green peas.

HYDERABADI MUTTON BIRYANI

Ingredients

- 400 gms basmati rice
- 500 gms mutton
- 115 gms onions
- 3 cloves of garlic
- 1" piece of ginger
- 4-5 red chillies
- 5 gms green chillies
- 1 lime
- 50 gms cashewnuts
- 225 gms curd
- 100 ml milk
- A small bunch coriander leaves
- 115 gms oil
- 1 pinch turmeric powder
- 2 gms each of cardamoms, cinnamon, cloves
- 2 bay leaves
- A few mint leaves
- A few strands of saffron soaked in milk
- Salt to taste

Method

- Clean and wash the mutton and cut into small pieces.
- Clean, wash and soak the rice. Keep aside.
- Slice the onions, coriander and mint leaves. Grind the ginger, red chillies and garlic into a fine paste.
- Heat oil and fry the onions till golden brown. Add the ground masala and the meat and fry.
- Add water and cook till the meat is tender and the gravy is thick.
- Add salt and boil rice till it is ¾th cooked.
- Tie the curd in a muslin cloth till the water drains out. Powder the cinnamon, cloves and cardamom and add to the curd.

- Also add turmeric powder, finely chopped green chillies, lime juice, coriander leaves and mint leaves to the curd.
- Now add this curd to the mutton.
- In a heavy bottom pan, put layers of rice, mutton and fried onions. Repeat the layers till all the rice and mutton are used up. Add saffron soaked in milk.
- Seal the lid with dough and bake for 20-30 minutes.
- Garnish with fried onion slices and cashewnuts and serve hot.

KODI VEPUDU *(A boneless chicken preparation)*

Ingredients

- 1 kg boneless chicken, cut into 1" cubes
- 500 gms diced onions
- 200 gms tomatoes, chopped
- 3 tsp ginger-garlic paste
- 1 tsp crushed black peppercorns
- 15 curry leaves
- ½ tsp turmeric powder
- ½ tsp red chilli powder
- 2-3 tsp coriander powder
- 2" piece cinnamon
- 5 green cardamoms
- 4 cloves
- 3 tbsp oil
- 25 gms cashewnuts
- Salt to taste

Method

- Heat oil in a kadai, add cinnamon, cardamom and cloves. After 10 seconds, add the onions and fry till golden brown.
- Add the ginger-garlic paste, tomatoes, turmeric, coriander powder and chilli powder. Cook for three minutes.
- Add the chicken cubes with enough water to prevent it from burning. Cook until the chicken is tender and the masala has dried.
- Add curry leaves, cashewnuts and pepper powder. Stir and cook for two minutes. Serve hot.

RICE PAYASAM

Ingredients

- 1 cup broken rice
- ½ cup grated jaggery
- 2½ cups thin coconut milk
- 1 cup thick coconut milk
- 1 tsp ground cardamoms
- A few cashewnuts
- A few raisins

Method

- ❖ Clean and wash the rice. Cook it in the thin coconut milk till the rice becomes soft.
- ❖ Add jaggery and stir till it dissolves.
- ❖ Roast the cashewnuts and raisins separately and keep aside.
- ❖ Pour in the thick coconut milk and bring to a boil, slowly.
- ❖ Remove from fire and garnish with cashewnuts, raisins and cardamom powder.

KADALE BELE PAYASAM
(Chana dal and coconut milk sweet dish)

Ingredients

- 2 cups of coconut milk
- 2 cups milk
- 2½ cups jaggery, grated
- ½ cup chana dal
- 50 gms cashewnuts
- 1 tbsp raisins
- 1 tsp cardamom powder

Method

- ❖ Boil the chana dal till it is soft.
- ❖ Fry the cashewnuts and keep aside.
- ❖ Grind the cooked chana dal into a smooth paste.
- ❖ Add milk and coconut milk and cook the dal paste till it is thick.

- ❖ Add the jaggery and cook for a few minutes, stirring continuously.
- ❖ Remove from fire and add the cardamom powder.
- ❖ Garnish with cashewnut pieces and raisins.

SWEET PONGAL ***(A rice and jaggery sweet dish)***

Ingredients

- 1½ cup rice
- ½ cup condensed milk
- 60 gms jaggery
- 3 cloves, powdered
- 3 pods cardamoms, powdered
- 2 tbsp ghee
- 1 tbsp cashewnuts, chopped
- 1 tbsp raisins
- 3 cups water

Method

- ❖ Heat the ghee in a kadai. Fry cashewnuts and raisins separately till golden brown. Remove and keep aside.
- ❖ In a pan, cook the rice. When the water has almost evaporated, add the jaggery and condensed milk. Simmer over low heat. When the mixture is almost dry, add the powdered cardamoms and cloves.
- ❖ Add the raisins and cashewnut pieces.
- ❖ Serve hot.

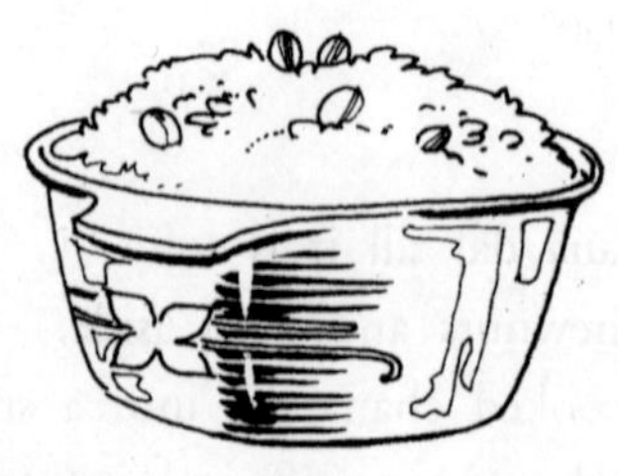

MYSORE PAK *(A gramflour sweet dish)*

Ingredients

- 2 cups sugar
- 1 cup gramflour
- ½ cup water
- 2 cups ghee

Method

- ❖ Heat 1 tablespoon ghee in a pan. Add gramflour and roast it till it emits a nice aroma. Set aside.
- ❖ In a pan gently warm sugar and water and make a syrup. Remove from heat, add the roasted gram flour and mix well.
- ❖ Return the pan to heat and keep stirring on low heat and put in spoonfuls of ghee. When the mix begins to bubble and the ghee separates, quickly spread on to a plate and drain out excess ghee.
- ❖ While still hot, cut into cubes.

MYSORE PAK *(A gramflour sweet dish)*

Ingredients

[illegible]

Method

- [illegible] add gramflour and [illegible] aroma. Set aside.
- [illegible] sugar and water [illegible] roasted gram [illegible] [illegible]
- [illegible] [illegible] plate and drain the excess ghee.
- While still hot, cut into cubes.

Chapter-3

The Western Splendour

From the coastal fringe of the South to the Western ghats, the cuisine undergoes a dramatic change. The dry and arid land of Rajputs, where the tales of valour mingle with the spicy flavours of local cuisine, is also famous for the beautiful palaces and colourful clothes. The dusty dunes of the Thar desert where vegetation is scarce, calls for imaginative cooking without much use of vegetables. The dishes created out of fenugreek seeds and onions have to be tasted to be believed. The climate is harsh and extreme so the cuisine has to suit the vagaries of Nature.

The land of *garba*, famous for the mirror embroidered clothes, is also known for its distinctive flavours. A pinch of sugar is found in almost every culinary creation. The tongue tickling *khaman dhokla* and the variety of *farsans* have a formidable reputation.

From the land of Marathas come a variety of culinary treats like *puran poli, bharali vangi* and *chikkis*. The *modaks* that are a special festive treat during *Ganesh Chaturthi* are a gourmand's delight. With a rich crop of groundnuts in the State, it is no wonder that the nut is used liberally in many dishes. Coconut is also used in some dishes and it could be due to the easy availability of this item all along the coast-line of Maharashtra.

Goan cooking has been highly influenced by the Portuguese and there is a liberal use of vinegar. A generous use of fish and meats, especially pork, has pervaded even the modest kitchens of Goa. The famous *vindaloos, sorpotel* and many other fish preparations have taken the world of cuisine by storm. The Goan cooking lies side-by-side with the Konkan cooking. But there is a distinct difference between the two. The Konkanis have a strong Maharashtrian influence and this can also be noticed in their food habits.

DHANIA ALOO MANGODI

(Coriander-potato-dal vadi preparation)

Ingredients

- 12 baby potatoes with the skin, blanched
- 150 gms mangodi, urad dal vadi
- 250 gms coriander leaves
- 3 tbsp ghee
- Oil for deep frying mangodi
- 1 large tomato
- 2 tsp ginger paste
- 1 tsp garlic paste
- 1 cup tomato (pureed)
- 2 tsp cumin seeds
- 3 tsp coriander powder
- 1 tsp chilli powder
- 3 tsp turmeric powder
- ½ tsp black pepper, coarsely powdered
- ½ tsp green cardamom powder
- ¼ tsp cinnamon powder
- ¼ nutmeg powder
- A generous pinch kasuri methi powder

For The Garnishing

- 1 tomato, julienned
- A few sprigs coriander leaves

Method

- Heat oil in a kadai and deep-fry the mangodi till golden. Remove on to an absorbent paper to drain excess oil. Reserve in a panful of water.
- Heat ghee in a kadai. Add cumin seeds, when they crackle add ginger-garlic paste. Fry well. Add the chopped coriander leaves and fry till the moisture evaporates.
- Add the coriander powder, chilli powder and turmeric powder. Mix well. Then add the tomato puree and fry until the ghee floats on top.
- Add potatoes, mangodi and salt. Fry till well coated.
- Sprinkle pepper, cardamom, cinnamon, nutmeg and kasuri methi powder over it. Stir well and remove from heat.
- Serve hot, garnished with coriander leaves and tomato.

KAKADI-TURIYA NU SHAK

(A light dish made with cucumber and ridge gourd)

Ingredients

- ½ kg cucumbers
- ½ kg ridge gourd (torai)
- ½ tsp cumin seeds
- 2 green chillies, ground
- 1½ tbsp ghee
- A pinch of soda bicarb
- Salt to taste

Method

- ❖ Peel and cut the vegetables into small pieces.
- ❖ Heat ghee in a pan and temper it with cumin seeds.
- ❖ Add the vegetables, soda bicarb, salt and sauté well.
- ❖ Add a little water and cook till done.
- ❖ Add the chilli paste, boil for 2 minutes and remove from heat.

PANEER MIRCHIWALI

(A spicy cottage cheese delicacy from Jodhpur)

Ingredients

- 200 gms paneer
- 10-12 green chillies
- 2 onions, chopped
- 2 big tomatoes
- 1 tbsp ginger-garlic paste
- 3 dry red chillies
- 1 tsp cumin seeds
- 2 tbsp oil
- ½ tsp garam masala
- Some chopped coriander leaves

Method

- ❖ Chop onions. Slit whole green chillies. Soak and make a paste of dry red chillies.
- ❖ Heat oil. Put cumin seeds and fry onions till lightly brown. Add ginger-garlic paste, red chilli paste, tomatoes and whole green chillies.
- ❖ Fry till this masala leaves the sides of the pan. Add salt and garam masala.
- ❖ Put the paneer and cook for 2-3 minutes.
- ❖ Remove from heat and serve hot garnished with coriander leaves.

GATTE KI SABJI

(A famous gramflour dish from Rajasthan)

Ingredients

- 1 cup gramflour
- 1 cup curd
- 2 tbsp oil
- 1½ tsp coriander powder
- 1 tsp red chilli powder
- ½ tsp turmeric powder
- ½ tsp black pepper, coarsely ground
- ½ tsp cumin seeds
- ½ tsp aniseed
- 1 tsp coriander seeds
- ½ tsp garam masala
- A pinch asafoetida
- 2 tbsp chopped coriander leaves
- Salt to taste

Method

- Mix gramflour, ½ tablespoon salt, 2 teaspoon oil, ¼ teaspoon each cumin, aniseed, coriander seeds and black pepper. Mix till it looks like bread-crumbs. Knead it with some water.
- Divide this dough into 4 parts. Roll each portion into a cylindrical way.
- Boil sufficient water in a deep pan. Put these gattas in it. Cover and leave for 10 minutes on medium heat. Allow to cool. Cut into small roundels. Reserve the boiled water for making the gravy.
- Heat oil in a pan. Add cumin, aniseed and asafoetida. Make a paste of the rest of the four spices with two tablespoon water.
- Add this masala paste to the oil, fry. Add curd and fry till the oil separates. Now add 2 cups of the reserved water and boil.
- Place the gattas in this gravy and simmer for 10 minutes. Sprinkle garam masala and coriander leaves. Serve hot.

KANDE KI SABJI

(Baby onions in thick and spicy gravy)

Ingredients

- 24 small-sized onions
- 2 medium-sized onions
- 150 gms tomatoes, chopped fine
- 2 tsp each of ginger and garlic paste
- 1 cup curd
- 1 tsp cumin seeds
- 1 tsp coriander powder
- 1 tsp turmeric powder
- 1 tsp chilli powder
- A generous pinch of amchoor powder
- A pinch of black pepper powder
- A pinch of black cardamom powder
- A pinch of cumin powder
- A generous pinch of bay leaf powder
- 2 green chillies, slit
- Some coriander leaves, chopped
- Salt to taste
- Oil for cooking

For The Filling

- 1½ tsp thin tamarind pulp
- 1 tsp amchoor powder
- ½ tsp coriander powder
- ½ tsp cumin powder
- ½ tsp chilli powder
- ½ tsp turmeric powder
- A generous pinch of black salt

Method

- ❖ Peel the small-sized onions and make criss-cross incisions on the top of each onion.
- ❖ Chop the medium-sized onions into small pieces and keep aside.
- ❖ Mix all the ingredients for the filling and put equal quantities of the filling between the incisions of the onions. Keep aside for half an hour.
- ❖ Heat a little oil in a frying pan and add the stuffed onions. Shallow fry over medium heat until pink in colour.
- ❖ To prepare the gravy, put the curd in a bowl. Add coriander powder, turmeric powder, chilli powder and whisk till it is nicely blended.

- ❖ Heat oil and add cumin seeds. When they begin to crackle, add the chopped onions. Sauté until brown. Add the ginger-garlic paste and fry till done. Stir in the curd mixture and cook till the oil floats on top. Add tomatoes and fry for 3 minutes.
- ❖ Place the stuffed onions in the gravy and cook for 3 minutes. Add 1½ cups of water, simmer over low heat, stirring occasionally until the gravy is reduced to half its quantity.
- ❖ Sprinkle the remaining ingredients. Garnish with coriander leaves and slit green chillies. Serve hot.

PAPAD CURRY

Ingredients

- 10 papads
- 1 large onion paste
- 3-4 cloves garlic paste
- 2 tbsp curd
- ½ tsp cumin seeds
- 1 tsp red chilli powder
- 2 tsp coriander powder
- ½ tsp turmeric powder
- ½ tsp garam masala powder
- Some coriander leaves, chopped
- 2 tbsp oil
- Salt to taste

Method

- ❖ Break the papads into small pieces. Lightly fry in oil and keep aside.
- ❖ Heat oil in a pan, add cumin seeds. When they begin to crackle, add the onion and garlic pastes. Fry till done.
- ❖ Add all four spices along with the curd. Fry till the oil separates. Add 2 cups of water and bring to a boil.
- ❖ Add the papad pieces and simmer for 2-3 minutes.
- ❖ Remove from fire.
- ❖ Garnish with coriander leaves and serve hot with chapatis.

METHI ALOO CHATPATA

(Hot and spicy fenugreek seeds with potatoes)

Ingredients

- 100 gms methi seeds
- 200 gms potatoes, diced
- 4 large onions, diced
- 1 cup milk
- 50 gms raisins
- 1½ tsp coriander powder
- ½ tsp turmeric powder
- ½ tsp red chilli powder
- A few almonds
- Oil for cooking

Grind Together

- 1" piece of ginger
- 6-8 cloves of garlic
- 2 green chillies
- 2 black cardamoms
- 2 green cardamoms
- 1 tsp peppercorns
- A big stick of cinnamon
- 4 cloves

Method

- ❖ Soak the methi seeds in 1 cup milk overnight. Boil them in the morning till the milk dries up.
- ❖ Soak the raisins for half an hour. Drain, keep aside.
- ❖ Fry the potatoes and keep aside.
- ❖ Heat oil in a karahi, fry the ground masalas, add turmeric powder, red chilli powder and coriander powder. Add salt.
- ❖ Add the chopped onions and fry till golden brown. Add the boiled methi seeds and fried potatoes. Cook on slow fire till the methi seeds are soft.
- ❖ Garnish with almonds and serve hot with puris.

MASALEWALI ALOO WADI
(Spicy lentil 'wadis' with potatoes)

Ingredients

- 500 gms potatoes, diced
- 2 dry masala wadis
- 2 onions, chopped
- 2 tomatoes, pureed
- 1 tbsp ginger-garlic paste
- ½ tsp red chilli powder
- ½ tsp turmeric powder
- ½ tsp black pepper powder
- ½ tsp coriander powder
- ½ tsp kasuri methi powder
- ½ tsp garam masala powder
- 2 green chillies, slit and deseeded
- Some coriander leaves, chopped
- 100 gms oil
- Salt to taste

Method

- Heat some oil in a pan and fry the wadis till golden brown. Remove and keep aside.
- Fry the chopped onions in the same oil, till light brown. Add the ginger-garlic paste, tomato puree and fry till the oil floats on top.
- Add red chilli powder, turmeric powder, black pepper powder, coriander powder, garam masala, salt and a cup of water. Mix well. Fry for 3 minutes.
- Add the potatoes, kasuri methi powder and cook them until the potatoes are tender.
- Add the fried wadis, 2 cups water and cook on slow fire for 5 minutes.
- Garnish with coriander leaves and green chillies.
- Serve hot.

VALACHI USAL *(A dried bean preparation)*

Ingredients

- 1 cup vaal, (dried butter beans)
- ½ tsp mustard seeds
- ½ tsp chilli powder
- ½ tsp turmeric powder
- A small piece of jaggery
- ¼ coconut, grated
- A bunch of coriander leaves
- Oil for frying
- Salt to taste

Method

- Soak the vaal overnight. Drain the water and tie the vaal in a clean muslin cloth. Keep in a moist place and let it sprout for 2 days.
- Cook the sprouted vaal and keep aside.
- Heat oil in a frying pan, add mustard seeds. When the mustard seeds crackle, add cooked vaal, salt, chilli powder, turmeric powder, jaggery and mix well. Cook for a few minutes.
- Garnish with chopped coriander leaves and grated coconut.
- Serve hot with rice.

BHARALI VANGI

(Brinjals stuffed with Maharashtrian peanut-coconut masala)

Ingredients

- 500 gms small green brinjals
- 200 gms groundnuts, roasted and peeled
- 3-4 tbsp grated coconut
- 1 pod garlic
- 1 large onion, chopped
- 2 large tomatoes, chopped
- ½ tsp garam masala powder
- ½ tsp turmeric powder
- ½ tsp coriander powder
- ½ tsp chilli powder
- Oil for cooking
- Salt to taste

Method

- Roast and peel the groundnuts and grind along with the garlic and coconut into a fine paste. Mix with the coriander powder, garam masala and salt. Keep aside.
- Remove the stalk and make deep criss-cross incisions on the top of the brinjals. Parboil them in salted water. Drain the water and keep aside.
- Fill the groundnut masala into the incisions made in the brinjals.
- Heat oil and fry the brinjals till light brown. Keep aside.

- ❖ Heat oil in a pan, add sliced onions and fry till golden brown. Add the tomatoes and turmeric powder. Fry till the oil floats on top. Add a little water to form a thick gravy.
- ❖ Drop the brinjals into the gravy and cook for 2 minutes.
- ❖ Garnish with coriander leaves and serve hot.

OONDHIU *(A mixed vegetable preparation)*

Ingredients

- 250 gms potatoes
- 225 gms sweet potatoes
- 225 gms small brinjals
- 115 gms yam
- 3 ripe bananas
- 1 bunch methi leaves
- 1 bunch coriander leaves, chopped
- 115 gms beans
- 115 gms double beans (papdi)
- 115 gms gramflour
- ½ coconut
- 1" piece of ginger, ground
- 8-10 cloves garlic
- 3-4 green chillies
- 1 lemon
- 2 tsp chilli powder
- ½ tsp turmeric powder
- 2 tsp sugar
- A pinch of soda bicarb
- ¼ tsp asafoetida
- Oil for cooking
- Salt to taste

Method

- ❖ Peel yam, potatoes, sweet potatoes. Cut the yam and sweet potatoes into 1" pieces.
- ❖ Remove the stems from the brinjals. Cut bananas into two pieces each, without removing the skin. Slit the potatoes, brinjals and bananas into quarters, half way down, only.
- ❖ Clean methi leaves, sprinkle with salt and keep aside.
- ❖ Clean the double beans and string the beans.
- ❖ Mix salt, a pinch of turmeric, chilli powder, a little oil, methi leaves and gramflour. Add a little water to form a stiff paste. Make balls from this paste. Fry till brown and keep aside.

- ❖ Mix together, grated coconut, chopped coriander leaves, garlic, ground ginger, green chillies, sugar, soda bicarb and asafoetida. Mix well. Divide into three portions.
- ❖ Stuff slit brinjals, potatoes and bananas with two portions. Smear yam and sweet potatoes with the remaining portion, setting aside about 1 teaspoon of the masala.
- ❖ Heat oil in a shallow pan, add masala and fry well. Add 300 ml water. When it boils, add double beans, beans and a pinch of soda. Cook for a few minutes.
- ❖ Add stuffed brinjals and cook for 10 minutes. Add potatoes, sweet potatoes and yam cubes. When nearly done, add fried gram balls and stuffed bananas. Cook till done. Serve hot.

BHINDANI KADHI

(Ladyfingers in a curd based gravy)

Ingredients

- 225 gms bhindi
- 250 ml buttermilk
- ½ tsp gramflour
- 1" piece ginger
- 2 green chillies
- ½ tsp mustard seeds
- 1 tsp turmeric powder
- A few coriander leaves
- Oil for cooking
- Salt to taste

Method

- ❖ Make a paste of gramflour with 1 teaspoon of buttermilk. Cut the bhindi into 1" pieces. Add salt and fry in hot oil.
- ❖ Heat a little oil, add mustard seeds. When they crackle, add buttermilk, chopped ginger, green chillies, coriander leaves, gramflour paste and salt.
- ❖ Heat gently until mixture thickens. Stir continuously, but lightly to prevent any lumps.
- ❖ Add the fried bhindi pieces and cook for a few minutes.
- ❖ Garnish with coriander leaves and serve hot.

BHARWA KARELA *(Stuffed bitter gourd delicacy)*

Ingredients

- 8 medium-sized karelas
- 3 potatoes
- 1 tomato
- 2 medium-sized onions
- 2 green chillies
- ½ tsp turmeric powder
- 1 tsp garam masala powder
- 1 tsp chilli powder
- 1 lemon
- Oil for frying
- Salt to taste

Method

- ❖ Boil the potatoes. Scrape off the scaly skin of the karelas and keep them immersed in salt water for half an hour.
- ❖ Drain off the water and slit the karelas lengthwise on one side. Apply a little salt on the insides and keep aside for a few minutes.
- ❖ Peel and mash the boiled potatoes.
- ❖ Chop onions, tomato and green chillies.
- ❖ Heat oil in a frying pan, add chopped onions, green chillies and fry for a while.
- ❖ Add turmeric powder, garam masala powder, chilli powder, salt and fry for a few minutes.
- ❖ Add chopped tomatoes, mashed potatoes and fry well.
- ❖ Add the lemon juice before removing from the fire.
- ❖ Stuff karelas with this filling and tie with a string.
- ❖ Heat oil in a frying pan. Fry the stuffed karelas on all sides until done. Serve hot.

TOMATO MAHASHA
(Tomatoes stuffed with potato and lentils)

Ingredients

- 500 gms under-ripe tomatoes
- 100 gms onions
- 225 gms potatoes
- 225 gms masoor dal
- 2 green chillies
- 50 gms oil
- Flour for paste
- Salt to taste

Method

- ❖ Cut the top of the tomatoes and scoop them out. Place on a rack to drain.
- ❖ Boil and mash the dal and potatoes.
- ❖ Chop onions and chillies.
- ❖ Heat a little oil and fry the onions. Mix together with chillies and salt. Add to the mashed dal and potatoes.
- ❖ Cool the mixture and fill this in the tomatoes.
- ❖ Firmly press the stuffing. Seal the lid with flour paste.
- ❖ Heat oil in a pan, fry the tomatoes first on the sealed side. When brown, turn and fry the other side.
- ❖ Cook covered until the tomatoes are quite soft.

ARVI CHOPS *(Colocasia deep fried balls)*

Ingredients

- 225 gms arvi
- 55 gms coconut
- 55 gms gramflour
- 3 onions
- 2 whole red chillies
- 1" piece of ginger
- A pinch of soda bicarb
- Salt to taste
- Oil for frying

Method

- ❖ Clean the arvi and peel. Boil it in a little water and mash.
- ❖ Grind coconut, chillies, onions and ginger into a smooth paste.
- ❖ Heat a little oil and fry the ground paste in it. Add salt. Keep aside.
- ❖ Prepare a batter with the gramflour. Make balls out of the mashed arvi. Stuff the balls with a little of the fried coconut masala.
- ❖ Dip the balls in the batter and deep fry.
- ❖ Serve hot with mint chutney.

KHAMAN DHOKLA

(A spongy, sweet and tangy gramflour snack)

Ingredients

- 200 gms chana dal
- 75 gms urad dal
- 5 gms ginger
- 10 gms green chillies
- A pinch asafoetida
- 1 tsp sugar
- ½ tsp soda bicarb
- ½ tsp turmeric powder
- Salt to taste
- 100 gms oil

To Temper

- 50 gms oil
- 1 tsp mustard seeds

To Garnish

- 115 gms coconut
- 30 gms coriander leaves

Method

- Mix the dals and soak for six hours.
- Grind the dals to a fine paste. Grind together ginger and green chillies.
- Add ginger-chilli paste, salt, asafoetida, soda bicarb and sugar to the dal paste.
- Heat oil, pour into the mixture, mix well and keep aside for 12 hours.
- When fermented, do not stir. Remove gently from the side and put into a greased pan. Steam for 15-20 minutes.
- Heat oil, add mustard seeds and when they begin to crackle, pour over the dhokla.
- Garnish with grated coconut and chopped coriander leaves.

OSAMAN *(Sweet and sour lentil preparation)*

Ingredients

- 1 cup arhar dal
- ¼ cup jaggery
- Lemon-sized ball of tamarind
- A small piece of ginger
- 4 green chillies, chopped
- A few curry leaves
- A few coriander leaves
- 1 tsp chilli powder
- 1 tsp mustard seeds
- ½ tsp cumin seeds
- 4 cloves
- A small piece of cinnamon
- Oil for frying
- Salt to taste

Method

- Cook the arhar dal with turmeric powder.
- Drain off the water from the dal into another vessel. Add salt, jaggery and tamarind juice to the drained off water and allow to simmer on low fire for a few minutes.
- Add green chillies, chopped ginger.
- Heat a little oil, add mustard seeds and cumin seeds. When they begin to crackle, add cloves, cinnamon and curry leaves. Fry well and temper curry with this tempering.
- Garnish with chopped coriander leaves and serve hot.

HANDWO
(A steamed rice-lentil preparation from Gujarat)

Ingredients

- 1 cup rice
- $^{1}/_{3}$ cup chana dal
- $^{1}/_{3}$ cup moong dal
- $^{1}/_{3}$ cup arhar dal
- 1 cup sour curd
- 4 green chillies
- 1 tsp mustard seeds
- ½ tsp fenugreek seeds
- 1 tsp chilli powder
- ¼ tsp turmeric powder
- A pinch of asafoetida
- A few sprigs curry leaves
- A few sprigs of coriander leaves
- A pinch of soda bicarb
- Oil for frying
- Salt to taste

Method

- ❖ Clean the rice and dals. Mix and powder coarsely.
- ❖ Chop green chillies and beat the curd. Mix curd, chopped chillies, curry leaves, coriander leaves, soda bicarb, chilli powder, turmeric powder and salt with the rice and dal powder. Make a thick batter.
- ❖ Heat a little oil, add the mustard seeds. When they begin to crackle, add asafoetida and fenugreek seeds. Fry until golden brown. Remove from fire and add to the batter.
- ❖ Keep the batter aside for one hour to ferment.
- ❖ Grease a container, put the batter and steam it.
- ❖ Then place the cooked handwo in a moderately hot oven for a few minutes until a crust forms on top.
- ❖ Garnish with coriander leaves and serve hot.

MASALA BHATH

(A spicy rice preparation from Maharashtra)

Ingredients

- 2 cups rice
- 100 gms brinjals
- 1 tbsp grated copra
- ½ cup grated coconut
- ½ cup curd
- 4-5 cashewnuts
- 2 cloves
- A small piece cinnamon
- ½ tsp cumin seeds
- ½ tsp coriander seeds
- ½ tsp mustard seeds
- ½ tsp turmeric powder
- 2 red chillies
- ½ tsp sugar
- 1 bay leaf
- A few curry leaves
- A few sprigs coriander leaves
- ½ cup oil
- Salt to taste

Method

- ❖ Wash rice and soak in salty water.
- ❖ Roast coriander seeds, cumin seeds, red chillies and copra. Powder and keep aside.
- ❖ Heat oil in a frying pan, add the mustard seeds, cinnamon, cloves, bay leaf and curry leaves. Fry well.

- Add rice and fry for a few minutes. Add brinjals and fry for 3 minutes.
- Add 2½ cups water, powdered masala, sugar, salt and curd and cook till the rice is done.
- Remove from fire and serve hot, garnished with grated coconut and chopped coriander leaves.

KHANDVI *(Delicious gramflour rolls)*

Ingredients

- 115 gms gramflour
- 150 ml buttermilk (thick)
- 150 ml water
- 2 green chillies
- 1" piece ginger
- ½ tsp turmeric powder
- ½ tsp chilli powder
- Salt to taste
- 1 tbsp oil

For Tempering

- A pinch asafoetida
- 1 tsp oil
- 1 whole red chilli
- 1 tsp mustard seeds

For Garnish

- 2 tbsp grated coconut
- Some coriander leaves

Method

- Mix together buttermilk, gramflour and water.
- Grind chillies and ginger to a fine paste.
- Mix together the gramflour paste and the chilli-ginger paste.
- Add turmeric and salt. Make a smooth solution and cook until water is almost absorbed and a soft dough consistency is obtained.
- Grease plates with oil and spread the mixture as thinly as possible, while still hot.
- Cut into 1" strips. Grease a finger and roll each strip.
- Heat oil, add whole red chilli, mustard seeds and asafoetida. When the seeds crackle, pour over khandvi.
- Garnish grated coconut and chopped coriander leaves.

DAL KEEMA *(Spicy minced meat in lentil gravy)*

Ingredients

- 500 gms minced meat
- 100 gms chana dal, soaked for 1 hour
- 225 gms onions
- 20 gms ginger
- 10 gms garlic
- ½ coconut
- 1 tsp poppy seeds
- ½ tsp cumin seeds
- 2 tbsp coriander seeds
- 2 cloves
- 1" piece cinnamon
- 4 red chillies
- ½ tbsp turmeric powder
- 1 bunch fresh coriander leaves
- 1 tbsp tamarind pulp
- 5 tbsp oil
- Salt to taste

Method

- ❖ Roast and powder coriander seeds, cumin seeds and red chillies.
- ❖ Grind together ginger-garlic. Grind coconut and poppy seeds separately.
- ❖ Chop the onions finely.
- ❖ Put the minced meat into a vessel, add the masala powder, ginger-garlic paste, turmeric powder and chopped onions. Cook over moderate heat until the meat is tender.
- ❖ Add chana dal along with the water in which it was soaked. When the dal is cooked, add the coconut and poppy paste and salt, diluted in a cup of water. Simmer for half an hour.
- ❖ Add tamarind pulp and simmer for another 5-10 minutes. If the gravy gets thick, add some more water and bring to a boil.
- ❖ Add chopped coriander leaves, remove from fire.
- ❖ Heat a little oil in a pan, add 1 chopped onion, cloves and cinnamon. When onions get browned, pour a spoon of the gravy into the frying pan.
- ❖ Mix well and add to the curry.

PRAWN BAFFAD

(A special coastal prawn preparation)

Ingredients

- ¼ kg prawns, shelled
- 8 Kashmiri chillies
- 2 medium-sized onions, chopped
- 1 large tomato, chopped
- ½" piece ginger
- 2-3 cloves of garlic
- 12 peppercorns
- ½ tsp cumin seeds
- ½ tsp turmeric powder
- Salt, tamarind and vinegar to taste
- Oil for cooking

Method

- Clean and devein the prawns.
- Grind the chillies, cumin seeds, peppercorns, garlic, ginger and mix in the turmeric powder.
- Heat a little oil in a pan. Fry the onions till brown. Add tomato and fry till the oil floats on top.
- Add the ground masala and fry for 3 minutes. Add the prawns, salt, tamarind and vinegar. Cover and cook till the prawns are done.
- Garnish with coriander leaves and serve.

MUTTON PAPDI

(An unusual mutton and double beans preparation)

Ingredients

- 500 gms mutton
- 115 gms double beans (papdi)
- 115 gms potatoes
- 1 large onion
- 10 gms ginger
- 5 gms garlic
- 10 gms coriander seeds
- 5 gms whole red chillies
- 2 cloves
- 1" piece of cinnamon
- ½ tsp cumin seeds
- ½ tsp turmeric powder
- 30 ml oil
- Salt to taste

Method

- Clean and cut the mutton into 1" cubes. Peel and dice the potatoes. Wash the double beans.

- ❖ Roast and powder coriander seeds, cumin seeds, and whole red chillies.
- ❖ Peel and grind ginger and garlic into a smooth paste. Chop the onion.
- ❖ Put the mutton in a pan, add masala powder, ground ingredients, half the onion and salt. Cover with water and simmer until the mutton is tender.
- ❖ Add the potatoes and double beans. Simmer until the vegetables are tender and the gravy is thick.
- ❖ Remove from fire. Add chopped coriander leaves.
- ❖ Heat oil in a pan. Add the remaining onions, cloves and cinnamon. When the onion turns brown, add the mutton curry. Stir well for five minutes and remove from heat.
- ❖ Garnish with coriander leaves and serve hot.

WESTEND FISH CURRY *(Sour fish curry)*

Ingredients

- 500 gms fish
- 2 large onions
- A small piece of ginger
- ½ coconut
- ½ tsp turmeric powder
- 2 tbsp coriander seeds
- 3-4 green chillies
- 2 cloves of garlic
- 20 gms tamarind
- 1 pinch mustard seeds
- 3 whole red chillies
- 5 tbsp coriander leaves
- 6 tbsp oil
- Salt to taste

Method

- ❖ Clean and wash the fish and cut into pieces.
- ❖ Grind together coriander seeds, red chillies, ginger, garlic and coconut.
- ❖ Soak tamarind and extract the pulp.
- ❖ Chop green chillies and onions.
- ❖ Heat oil, add chopped green chillies and onion. Sauté for a few minutes.

- Add ground masala and fry well.
- Add the tamarind pulp and water along with salt. Bring to a boil.
- Add the fish and simmer until the fish is cooked.
- Garnish with chopped coriander leaves and serve hot with rice.

SAFED MAAS

(A curd-based meat curry from Rajasthan)

Ingredients

- 1 kg meat, cut into small pieces
- ¼ coconut
- 8 onions
- 5 pods garlic
- 1" piece ginger
- 6 green chillies
- ¼ kg curd
- 2 tbsp vinegar
- 2 eggs, hard boiled
- 3 large tomatoes
- 4 green cardamoms
- 4-5 bay leaves
- ¼ kg ghee
- Salt to taste

Grind Together

- 2 sticks cinnamon
- 8 green cardamoms
- 8 cloves
- 10-12 almonds
- 1 black cardamom
- Some coriander leaves
- 1 tsp poppy seeds

Method

- Grind 6 onions, ginger and garlic intc a smooth paste. Separately grind the coconut into a fine paste. Grind together the almonds and poppy seeds.
- Cut the hard boiled eggs into half.
- Heat the ghee and put whole spices. Add 2 chopped onions and brown lightly. Now add the onion, ginger, garlic paste and fry well.
- Add chopped green chillies, stir well and cook. Add the ground coconut, half of the curd, ground almonds and poppy seeds.

- When the masala is cooked, add meat, whole green chillies, salt, remaining curd and the garam masalas. Cook for 4 minutes.
- Add the tomatoes, and cook till the masalas are well blended.
- Garnish with hard boiled eggs and coriander leaves.

PATRA-NI-MACCHI

(Fish steamed in banana leaves)

Ingredients

- 500 gms pomfret
- Some banana leaves
- Salt to taste
- Oil for frying

For The Chutney, Grind To Paste

- 1 cup coconut, grated
- ½ cup coriander leaves
- 3-4 green chillies
- 2 cloves garlic
- ½ tsp cumin seeds
- 1 tsp sugar
- ½ tsp salt
- 1 tsp tamarind

Method

- Clean and cut the pomfret into 6 slices of 1" width. Rub with salt and keep aside.
- Cut pieces of banana leaves, avoiding the rib. The pieces should be large enough to wrap each slice of fish. Hold each piece of leaf, directly over a flame for a few seconds to soften it.
- Smear oil on one side of each piece of leaf. Coat each slice of fish with chutney. Lay one slice on the greased side of the leaf. Roll it up into a packet. Tie with a thread.
- Steam till the fish is cooked.
- Serve immediately in the wrapping.

MAKKI KA SOYTA

(A Rajasthani mutton preparation with corn kernels)

Ingredients

- ½ kg mutton
- ½ kg fresh corn kernels
- 115 gms curd
- 60 gms onions, ground
- 25 gms garlic, ground
- 240 ml milk
- 6-8 green chillies, chopped
- 60 gms gramflour
- 15 ml lime juice
- 6 cloves
- 1 tbsp cumin seeds
- 4 black cardamoms
- 2 long sticks of cinnamon
- 12 gms coriander seeds, powdered
- 2 bay leaves
- ½ tsp turmeric powder
- 1 tsp red chilli powder
- 15 gms sugar
- Some coriander leaves
- 175 gms ghee
- Salt to taste

Method

- Grate the fresh corn, coarsely. Keep aside.
- Heat the ghee, add cloves, black cardamom, cinnamon and bay leaves. Fry till they emanate a rich aroma.
- Add the meat along with the curd, salt, red chillies, coriander seeds, turmeric powder, cumin seeds, onions and garlic. Fry the meat until it is well browned.
- Add enough water and cook till the meat is almost tender.
- Add the grated corn kernels, green chillies, sugar, milk and gramflour and cook on medium heat, stirring frequently to avoid the kernels from sticking to the bottom of the pan.
- Add lime juice and coriander leaves and stir well. Remove from fire.
- Garnish with slit green chillies and serve.

MACKEREL MASALA
(Barbecued stuffed fish)

Ingredients

- 6 mackerels
- 3 onions, finely chopped
- ½ coconut, grated
- 2 tbsp ginger-garlic-red chilli paste
- 4 cloves
- 4 peppercorns
- 4 cinnamon pieces
- A few coriander seeds
- 1 tsp cumin seeds
- 1 tsp red chilli powder
- ¼ cup vinegar
- Juice of 1 lemon
- Oil for frying
- Salt to taste

Method

- Clean the mackerels, remove the heads and slit the sides.
- Marinate them in salt and lemon juice.
- Lightly fry the coconut along with cloves, peppercorns, cinnamon and coriander seeds till light brown.
- Add this to ginger-garlic-red chilli paste and grind to a smooth paste.
- Heat a little oil in a frying pan. Add the onions and sauté till translucent. Add the vinegar, red chilli powder, salt and mix well.
- Fill mackerels with this stuffing on both sides and spread it on the outside too. Tie a string around the fish.
- Barbecue or shallow fry.

PRAWN VINDALOO *(Goan prawn delicacy)*

Ingredients

- 500 gms prawns, shelled and washed
- 225 gms potatoes, parboiled and chopped
- 225 gms tomatoes, tomatoes
- 115 gms onions, chopped
- 2 tbsp oil

Grind in Vinegar

- A few garlic cloves
- 1" piece ginger
- 50 gms cumin seeds
- 5 gms mustard seeds
- 5 gms red chillies, deseeded
- ½ tsp turmeric powder
- Salt to taste

Method

- ❖ Smear half the quantity of the ground vinegar masala over the prawns and keep aside for 2 hours.
- ❖ Heat oil in a pan and fry onions till brown. Remove and keep aside.
- ❖ Now fry the prawns in the same oil, adding the remaining vinegar masala to it. Cook on a low flame till half done.
- ❖ Then add the tomatoes, fried onions and potatoes and cook on slow fire, adding water if necessary.
- ❖ Serve hot, garnished with slit green chillies.

CHICKEN VINDALOO

(The famous Goan chicken delight)

Ingredients

- 1 chicken

Grind Together

- 4 medium-sized onions
- 2 pods of garlic
- 10-12 Kashmiri red chillies
- 1 tbsp cumin seeds
- 2" piece of cinnamon
- ¼ cup vinegar
- Oil for frying
- Salt to taste

Method

- ❖ Clean and joint the chicken.
- ❖ Grind the masalas in vinegar and rub it on the chicken pieces.
- ❖ Chop the onions.
- ❖ Heat oil in a pan, add the onions and fry till they turn to a golden brown colour.
- ❖ Add the cinnamon and the chicken. Cook on slow fire till the chicken is tender.
- ❖ Add salt to taste.
- ❖ Serve hot, garnished with slit chillies.

Desserts

SHRIKHAND ***(Sweet, flavoured curd)***

Ingredients

- 500 gms curd
- 300 gms sugar
- 25-gms each of cashewnuts, almonds and pistachios
- 1 tbsp charoli
- 1 tsp cardamom powder
- A few strands of saffron dissolved in 1 tbsp warm milk

Method

- Tie the curd in a clean muslin cloth and let it hang for 2-3 hours so that the water drains out.
- Break the nuts into small pieces and keep aside.
- Mix the sugar with the solid curd until it is of a creamy consistency.
- Add the saffron, cardamon powder, and the nuts to the shrikhand. Serve chilled.

CHIKKI ***(Sugar and groundnut toffees)***

Ingredients

- 1 cup groundnuts
- ½ cup sugar
- 1 tbsp sesame seeds
- 1 tbsp butter

Method

- Roast the groundnuts and remove the peel. Break them into medium-sized pieces, and grease a thali.
- On slow fire, melt the sugar in a pan.
- Add the groundnut pieces and 1 tablespoon of butter. Add the sesame seeds. Mix quickly because sugar solidifies very quickly. Remove from fire.
- Topple the mixture into the thali and spread. Let it set. Cut into cubes with a sharp knife. When the chikki cools, separate the pieces and store in an airtight container.

CHOORMA LADDOO *(Sweet semolina balls)*

Ingredients

- 1 kg semolina
- ½ kg sugar
- ½ litre milk
- 1 kg ghee
- 50 gms charoli
- 20 gms powdered nutmeg
- ½ tsp salt

Method

- ❖ Fry the semolina in 250 gms ghee and mix with ½ litre milk.
- ❖ Add salt and keep the mixture aside for about 3½ hours so that the milk is completely absorbed by the semolina.
- ❖ Shape mixture into small balls and fry them in the rest of the ghee. Cool. Break the balls.
- ❖ Grind the sugar into a fine powder, add the nutmeg and charoli and mix with semolina.
- ❖ Add heated ghee to the mixture and mix well until the ingredients have blended. Shape into laddoos.

PURAN POLI
(Indian bread with the famous jaggery-based stuffing)

Ingredients

For The Dough

- ½ cup maida
- ½ cup semolina
- ¼ tsp salt
- Ghee for frying

For The Filling

- 1 cup chana dal
- ½ cup jaggery
- ¼ cup sugar
- 4-6 green cardamoms
- ¼ tsp salt

Method

- ❖ Sift the maida and semolina with the salt. Knead into a dough.

- ❖ Wash and soak the chana dal for half an hour. Powder the cardamoms.
- ❖ Take 1½ cups of water and cook the chana dal in a pressure cooker for about 15 minutes. Add jaggery, cardamom powder, salt and sugar to the chana and cook in a pan, over medium flame. Stir continuously.
- ❖ Cook the mixture till it stops sticking to the pan. Cool and grind into a smooth paste. Make even-sized balls from the dough. Form small katori from each ball and fill in the chana paste. Seal and roll out into chapatis.
- ❖ Fry the chapatis with ghee on both sides. Serve hot.

GUJIA

(Deep-fried packets made of flour stuffed with sweetened coconut)

Ingredients

- 1 cup maida
- 1 cup sugar
- ½ cup khoya
- ½ cup grated coconut
- 3 green cardamoms
- A few raisins, fried
- A few cashewnuts, fried
- A few almonds, chopped
- 1 pinch salt
- 2 tbsp ghee

Method

- ❖ Mix sugar and coconut and cook till the sugar melts. Powder the cardamoms and keep aside.
- ❖ Add khoya and fry till the mixture becomes dry.
- ❖ Add cardamom powder, nuts and the raisins to the khoya mixture. Cool the mixture.
- ❖ To maida, add salt, ghee and knead into a stiff dough. While rolling the dough and filling it, keep a wet cloth on the dough so that it doesn't dry.
- ❖ Roll into thin rounds, put the filling and seal the edges by putting some water on the edges and pressing.
- ❖ Heat ghee and deep fry the gujias.

GROUNDNUT BARFI

(A delicious groundnut sweetmeat)

Ingredients

- 250 gms groundnuts, roasted and coarsely powdered
- 250 gms sugar
- 1 cup water
- 50 gms coconut powder
- A few green cardamoms, powdered
- 1 tbsp ghee

Method

- In a pan, heat the sugar and water to make a 1-string syrup.
- Add groundnut powder, coconut powder and ghee along with the cardamom powder.
- Stir till the mixture leaves the side of the pan.
- Grease a thali with ghee and spread the mixture.
- Cut into barfis while the mixture is still hot.

Chapter-4

The Eastern Spread

Having covered the ground from the tip of the country to the foot, there is but one region that is left. The land of tigers, Durga puja, music and literature. Bengal is famous for its sweets and fish preparations. Every Indian has heard about and tasted the world famous *rosogolla.* The wide variety of fish preparations has baffled many fish lovers. Every part of the fish, including the head and eggs, is used for some dish or the other, in a creative manner. Bengali cuisine is not just sweets and fish. There are umpteen types of vegetarian and other non-vegetarian cuisine. An average Bengali is fond of good food.

No feast in a Bengali household is complete without the inclusion of several fish preparations and vegetarian delicacies. Weddings are a time of feasting. Mutton as well as several types of fish preparations are served along with *dals* and vegetables. Various types of sweets and chutneys are prepared in every Bengali household. Right from tomato to raw mango to papaya, there is a recipe for all kinds of chutneys, which are sweet and sour in taste.

The flavour is predominantly that of mustard. Unlike the other regions, Bengali vegetarian dishes do not require the addition of turmeric powder or the use of garlic. Onion is sparingly used. The tempering essentially consists of the *paanch phoron* which lends the dishes a typical flavour. Vegetables are cooked in a very simple manner so as to preserve their natural flavour. The use of spices is sparing and each dish has a particular preparation. Bengalis love all kinds of fries and most vegetables are fried, to be eaten as an accompaniment with rice and dal. Potato, karela, parwal, pumpkin, etc. are prepared and fried without using any spices except a touch of turmeric powder and salt. And, of course, the fish fry takes a place of honour in the menu.

ALOO PHOOL GOBHI

(Cauliflower and potato curry)

Ingredients

- 1 medium-sized cauliflower
- 2 large potatoes
- 1 tomato
- 2 green chillies
- 1 tbsp coriander and cumin seeds, ground to paste
- 1 bay leaf
- 1 tsp garam masala powder
- 1 tsp whole cumin seeds
- ½ tsp sugar
- 2 tsp ghee
- Salt to taste

Method

- Cut the cauliflower into large pieces, without its leaves. Cut the potatoes into rounded shapes and wash. Lightly fry both separately and remove.
- Put fresh oil in a kadai. When hot, add whole cumin and bay leaf. Mix the spices in a little water and add it to the oil and fry till it leaves the sides. Keep sprinkling water.
- Put the vegetables, already half-fried. Toss them in the spices.
- When they give off an aroma, add half a cup of water. Lower heat and simmer.
- Lastly add tomatoes, green chillies, salt and sugar. You may also add fresh green peas if you wish.
- Once the gravy is thick, add pure ghee and ground garam masala. Serve hot.

ALOOR DOM *(Stuffed potato curry)*

Ingredients

- 450 gms potatoes
- 225 gms green peas, mashed
- 3 medium-sized onions, chopped
- 2-3 green chillies
- Juice of 1 lemon
- 30 gms ghee
- Salt to taste

For The Gravy

- 2 medium-sized onions, chopped
- 225 gms tomatoes, pureed
- ½ tsp cumin seeds
- A pinch of asafoetida
- ½ tsp turmeric powder
- ½ tsp chilli powder
- Oil for cooking

Method

To Make The Stuffing

- Heat oil in a kadai. Add chopped onions, mashed peas, salt and cook until the peas are quite soft. Add a few drops of lemon juice.

To Make The Curry

- Heat oil in a kadai. Add chopped onions, chilli powder, turmeric powder and tomato puree.
- Add a little water and simmer until ready.
- Boil potatoes in jackets.
- Peel and cut the potatoes into half, lengthwise. Scoop out the centre, leaving ½" thick walls.
- Fill in with the prepared stuffing.
- Put the two sides together and stick with toothpicks.
- Fry until light brown. Put into the curry and cook for 15-30 minutes.
- Serve hot, garnished with chopped coriander leaves.

CHOCHORI *(A mixed vegetable preparation)*

Ingredients

- 225 gms potatoes
- 115 gms brinjals
- 115 gms pumpkin
- 115 gms green peas
- 4-5 green chillies
- ½ tsp turmeric powder
- 1 tsp sugar
- 1 whole red chilli
- 1 tsp of panch phoron
- 3 tbsp oil
- Salt to taste

For The Panch Phoron

- Kalonji
- Jeera
- Saunf
- Methi seeds
- Mustard seeds

(Combine these in equal proportions and keep in a jar. This mixed masala is used in most Bengali dishes for seasoning.)

METHOD

- ❖ Peel, clean and dice the vegetables into cubes. Shell the peas.
- ❖ Heat oil in a kadai. Break the whole red chilli into pieces. Add the chilli pieces and panch phoron. When they begin to crackle, add the vegetable pieces.
- ❖ Add turmeric powder, sugar and salt. Slit the green chillies and add. Stir fry the vegetables till the masalas are properly blended.
- ❖ Although this dish does not require any additional water to cook since the vegetables should cook in their natural juices, you may sprinkle a little water if required. Cover and simmer until the vegetables are tender and the water has evaporated.
- ❖ Charchari is a dry preparation, so avoid using too much water.
- ❖ Serve hot with rice. This dish goes very well with 'khichri'.

GHUGNI *(Spicy green peas)*

Ingredients

- 250 gms green peas
- ½ kg potatoes
- ½ tsp sugar
- 1 lemon
- 1" piece of ginger, julienned
- 1 tsp chilli powder
- 1 tsp cumin seeds
- 1 pinch of pepper powder
- 2 tbsp coconut, grated
- A few coriander leaves
- Oil to fry
- Salt to taste

Method

- Shell the green peas and boil in salted water. Drain and keep aside. Boil the potatoes separately. Peel, cut into pieces and keep aside.
- Heat oil in a kadai. Add cumin seeds, when they splutter add ginger juliennes.
- Add the boiled peas, potatoes, chilli powder, salt and sugar. Stir for a minute.
- Squeeze the juice of lemon over the ghugni, sprinkle the pepper and remove from fire.
- Garnish with coriander leaves and coconut.
- Serve hot as a snack.

ALOO POTOLER JHOL *(Parwal and potato curry)*

Ingredients

- 250 gms potol, parwal
- 2 potatoes
- 2 tomatoes
- 1" piece of ginger
- 1 tbsp coriander powder
- 1½ tsp cumin powder
- ½ tsp turmeric powder
- ½ tsp chilli powder
- ½ tsp cumin seeds
- 1 whole red chilli
- ½ tbsp sugar
- 1 bay leaf
- 1 tsp garam masala powder
- Salt to taste
- 3 tbsp oil

METHOD

- Cut the potol into half. Peel and dice the potatoes.
- Heat a little oil in a kadai and lightly fry the potol and potatoes separately. Keep aside.
- Grind the ginger into a smooth paste and blend with a teaspoon of water. To this paste, add the chilli powder, turmeric powder, cumin powder and coriander powder. Blend to form a thin paste with water.
- Heat oil, add cumin seeds and whole red chilli (broken into pieces). When they begin to crackle, add the masala paste along with the tomatoes. Fry till the tomatoes blend with the masala.

- Add the fried vegetables, sugar and salt. Pour about 3 cups of water and simmer on low heat till the vegetables are done. The gravy should be thick.
- Sprinkle garam masala and remove from fire.
- Serve hot with rice or chapatis.

BADHA KOPI DIYE CHALER JHAL

(A cabbage and rice preparation)

Ingredients

- 200 gms cabbage
- 120 gms potatoes
- 15 gms rice
- 100 gms onions
- 1" piece ginger
- 5 green chillies
- 1 tsp chilli powder
- 1 tsp sugar
- 1" piece cinnamon stick
- 3 cardamoms
- 2 cloves
- Salt to taste
- Oil for cooking

Method

- Shred the cabbage and steam.
- Soak the rice for 10 minutes.
- Peel and cut potatoes into small pieces.
- Slice the onion, ginger and green chillies finely.
- Heat the oil and fry the potatoes until light brown. Keep aside.
- In the same oil, fry the onions. Add the cloves, cardamoms and cinnamon. Stir for a minute.
- Add rice, chilli powder and ginger. Fry till the rice turns brown. Add sufficient water to cook the rice.
- When the rice is nearly cooked, add the cabbage, potatoes and green chillies. Simmer till the water has been absorbed.
- Add salt and sugar. Fry for about 5 minutes.
- Serve hot.

ALOO POSTO *(Potatoes with khus-khus)*

Ingredients

- ½ kg potatoes
- 2 tbsp khus-khus
- 2 green chillies
- 1 tsp salt
- 1 tsp sugar
- ¼ tbsp kalonji
- Oil for cooking

Method

- ❖ Peel and dice the potatoes.
- ❖ Soak the khus-khus for 30 minutes. Grind to a smooth paste along with green chillies.
- ❖ Heat oil in a kadai. Add kalonji. Add the potatoes and fry for a few minutes till they turn golden brown.
- ❖ Add the khus-khus paste, sugar and salt. Add a little water. Cover and cook till the potatoes are done. The dish is a dry preparation so don't add too much water.
- ❖ Serve hot with rice.

SHUKTO
(A mixed vegetable dish with mustard flavour)

Ingredients

- 4 potatoes
- 2 drumsticks
- 2 brinjals
- 2 sweet potatoes
- 2 raw bananas
- 1 bitter gourd
- 1 carrot
- 1 radish
- 1 cup milk
- 1" piece ginger
- 1 tbsp coriander seeds
- 2 tbsp mustard seeds
- 1 tbsp khus-khus
- ¼ tsp paanch phoron
- 1 tsp sugar
- 1 tbsp ghee
- 1 tbsp mustard oil
- Salt to taste

Method

- ❖ Wash and cut the brinjals into cubes. Scrape potatoes, carrot, radish, sweet potatoes, bananas and cut into large cubes.

- Scrape and cut bitter gourd into roundels. Apply salt and keep aside for half an hour. Pat dry after spreading it over a clean dry cloth.
- Heat oil in a kadai and fry the bitter gourd pieces till they are crisp. Remove and keep aside.
- Grind mustard seeds, coriander seeds, ginger and khus-khus into a thick paste.
- Heat oil and add paanch phoron. When it splutters, add the vegetables (except bitter gourd). Stir fry for a few minutes.
- Add the ground masala and two cups water. Cover and cook till the vegetables are almost cooked.
- Add the fried bitter gourd, salt and sugar. Cook till all the vegetables are tender.
- Remove from fire, add ghee. Serve hot.

BADHA KOPIR GHONTO

(A cabbage preparation)

Ingredients

- 400 gms cabbage
- 2 large potatoes
- 100 gms green peas, shelled
- 1 large tomato, chopped
- 1" piece ginger, ground
- 1 tsp coriander powder
- 2 tsp cumin powder
- 1 bay leaf
- ½ tsp turmeric powder
- ½ tsp cumin seeds
- ½ tsp garam masala powder
- 1 tsp ghee
- 1 tsp sugar
- 2 tbsp oil
- Salt to taste

Method

- Finely chop the cabbage, dice the potatoes into even-sized pieces and shell the peas.
- Heat oil in a kadai. Drop the potatoes in it and fry till lightly brown. Remove and keep aside.
- Heat some more oil in a kadai and add the cumin seeds, ground ginger and bay leaf. Stir till the cumin seeds splutter.

- ❖ Mix turmeric, coriander and cumin powders in a tablespoon of water and pour it into the oil. Fry for 2 minutes (add water in case it begins to burn).
- ❖ Add the cabbage, stir for a few minutes. Add green peas and cover. Cook until the cabbage is tender.
- ❖ Add the fried potatoes, tomato, salt and sugar. Cook until the vegetables are done. Add garam masala and a dollop of ghee. Remove from heat and serve hot.

BEGUN BHAJA ***(Brinjal fry)***

Ingredients

- 2 large, round, seedless brinjals
- 2 tsp turmeric powder
- Salt to taste
- Oil for frying

Method

- ❖ Cut the brinjals into ½" roundels.
- ❖ Coat the pieces with salt and turmeric powder.
- ❖ Heat oil in a kadai. Deep fry the brinjals on both sides until they are brown.
- ❖ Serve hot with rice and dal. (The same method can be used to make potato fry, parwal fry and karela fry)

DOI BEGUN ***(Fried brinjals in curd)***

Ingredients

- 6 medium-sized brinjals
- 1 cup curd
- 1 onion
- 3 green chillies
- ¼" piece of ginger
- 1 clove garlic, crushed
- ½ tsp turmeric powder
- ½ tsp chilli powder
- ¼ tsp mustard seeds
- ½ tsp cumin seeds
- Some curry leaves
- Salt to taste
- Oil for frying

Method

- Chop the green chillies finely, jullienne the ginger and slice the onions.
- In a large bowl, beat the curd with a teaspoon of salt and keep aside.
- Cut the brinjals into long strips. Make a mixture of salt, chilli powder and turmeric powder. Coat the brinjals with the mixture.
- Heat oil in a kadai and deep fry the brinjal pieces. Remove and keep aside.
- In another kadai, heat a little oil and add the mustard seeds. When the mustard seeds begin to splutter, add cumin seeds, ginger julliennes, green chillies, onion, garlic and curry leaves. Fry them for some time.
- Temper the beaten curd with the fried ingredients.
- Slip the fried brinjals into the tempered curd and let them soak the flavours.
- Serve with rice or pulao.

KACHA KOLAR JHAL ***(A raw banana preparation)***

Ingredients

- 4-5 raw bananas
- 1 large potato
- 1 large tomato
- 1 large onion
- 1" ginger
- 5-6 cloves of garlic
- 1 tsp cumin seeds
- ½ tsp mustard seeds

- 1 tsp coriander powder
- ½ tsp turmeric powder
- 1 tsp red chilli powder
- 2-3 green chillies
- ½ tsp garam masala powder
- 1 bay leaf
- Salt to taste
- Oil for cooking

Method

- Peel the raw bananas and the potatoes. Cut them into 1" pieces.
- Grind together ginger, garlic, cumin seeds and green chillies into a fine paste.
- Chop the onion and tomato finely.
- Mix the masala paste, turmeric powder, chilli powder, and coriander powder in a tablespoon of water. Blend well.
- Heat oil in a kadai, add the mustard seeds and bay leaf. When the seeds begin to crackle, add the onion and fry till they turn light brown.
- Add the masala paste and the tomato. Fry until the oil floats on top.
- Add the raw bananas, potato, salt and enough water for cooking. Cover and cook over medium heat until the vegetables are almost cooked. Add half a cup water and simmer over low heat until the gravy thickens.
- Garnish with fresh coriander leaves and serve.

CHOLAR DAL *(Chana dal)*

Ingredients

- 1 cup chana dal
- 1 tsp ginger paste
- ½ tsp cumin seeds
- 2 bay leaves
- 2 whole red chillies
- 1" cinnamon piece
- 3-4 cardamoms
- 3 cloves
- 1 tsp turmeric powder
- 1 tsp sugar
- ¼ coconut, sliced thinly
- 3 tbsp ghee
- A few coriander leaves, chopped
- Salt to taste

Method

- ❖ Clean and wash the dal.
- ❖ Chop the coconut slices. Fry them in a little ghee till they are light brown. Remove and keep aside.
- ❖ Boil the chana dal, turmeric powder, salt and sugar. Add just enough water to get a thick consistency.
- ❖ Heat ghee in a kadai, add cumin seeds, bay leaf, whole garam masala and whole red chillies. When they begin to crackle add slit green chillies and ginger paste. Stir for a minute and pour in the dal.
- ❖ Add the fried coconut bits. Allow to simmer for about 5 minutes, stirring occasionally. Pour the ghee on it and remove from heat.
- ❖ Garnish with coriander leaves and serve hot.

MOOGER DAL *(Moong dal)*

Ingredients

- 1 cup moong dal
- 2 green chillies
- ½ tsp cumin seeds
- 2 bay leaves
- 1 tsp sugar
- ¼ tsp turmeric powder
- 1 tsp ghee
- A few sprigs of coriander leaves
- Salt to taste

Method

- ❖ Clean and wash the moong dal. Drain, spread on a clean dry cloth and let the moisture dry.
- ❖ Roast the dal in a kadai till it is golden brown and emanates a flavour.
- ❖ Boil the dal with turmeric powder, in 2 cups of water, till it gets cooked. Don't overcook the dal, the grains should remain intact.
- ❖ Add sugar, slit green chillies and salt. Simmer for a few minutes.
- ❖ Heat ghee in a kadai and add cumin seeds and bay leaves. When the cumin seeds begin to splutter, add the dal.
- ❖ Garnish with coriander leaves and serve hot.

DHOKAR DALNA *(Lentil cubes and potato curry)*

Ingredients

- 250 gms chana dal
- 3 large potatoes
- 3 tsp ginger paste
- 3 tsp cumin seeds
- 3 green chillies
- ½ tsp turmeric powder
- 1 sprig coriander leaves
- ½ tsp garam masala powder
- Salt to taste
- Oil for frying

Method

- Soak the dal overnight. Drain the water and grind into a fine paste.
- Cut the potatoes into cubes and fry lightly.
- Grind the cumin seeds into a fine paste.
- Make a batter of the dal, salt and chilli powder.
- Grease a thali and pour this batter into it. Steam it for a while. When the dal cools, cut it into small square pieces.
- Heat oil in a kadai. Fry the dal pieces and keep aside.
- In another kadai, heat a little oil and add ginger paste. Dissolve the turmeric powder, chilli powder in a teaspoon of water. Add this paste along with the cumin paste to the oil. Fry till the moisture evaporates.
- Add potatoes and stir for about 5 minutes. Pour 2 cups of water and bring to a boil. Add the fried dal pieces and cook over low heat for about 10 minutes.
- When the potatoes are cooked, add garam masala powder.
- Garnish with green chillies and coriander leaves.
- Serve hot with rice.

TOMATOR CHATNI *(Tomato chutney)*

Ingredients

- ½ kg red and ripe tomatoes
- ½ kg sugar
- 1 pinch of paanch phoron
- 2 whole red chillies
- ¼ tsp red chilli powder
- 1 bay leaf
- A few raisins
- 1 tsp salt
- 1 tsp oil

Method

- Cut the tomatoes into small pieces.
- Heat a little oil in a kadai. Add the bay leaf, whole red chillies and the paanch phoron. When the mustard seeds begin to crackle, add the tomato pieces and sugar. Cover and cook for a few minutes. You may add water if you want a thin gravy.
- Add red chilli powder, salt and raisins. Cook on low heat until the tomatoes turn dark red in colour and the gravy is thick.

MANGSHER JHOL *(Mutton curry)*

Ingredients

- 1 kg mutton
- 225 gms onions
- 225 gms potatoes
- 2 large tomatoes
- 1 tsp turmeric powder
- 1 tsp red chilli powder
- 1 tsp sugar
- 1 tbsp ginger paste
- 1 bay leaf
- 4-5 cloves
- 3 cardamoms
- 1" stick of cinnamon
- A few peppercorns
- 4 tbsp oil
- Salt to taste

Method

- Grind one onion into a paste. Chop the rest of the onions and tomatoes finely. Keep aside.
- Marinate the mutton pieces in a little salt and onion paste for about an hour.
- Peel and dice the potatoes into cubes.
- Heat some oil and fry the potatoes till light brown in colour. Keep aside.
- In a tablespoon of water, add the ginger paste, turmeric powder, chilli powder and make a thick paste.
- Heat a little oil in the pressure pan. Add the cinnamon, cloves, cardamoms, bay leaf and peppercorns.
- Add the onions and tomatoes. Fry till the oil floats on top. Add the masala paste and fry for a few minutes.
- Add the marinated mutton along with salt and sugar. Fry until the meat is quite dry.
- Add about 2 cups of water and pressure cook until the mutton is almost done.
- Open the cooker and add the fried potatoes to the curry. Cook until done.
- Garnish with coriander leaves and serve hot.

BHAPA ILISH *(Steamed Hilsa)*

Ingredients

- 1 kg fish (Hilsa)
- 2 green chillies
- 2 tbsp sour curd
- 100 gms mustard seeds
- ½ tsp turmeric powder
- ½ tsp red chilli powder
- 2 tbsp mustard oil
- Salt to taste

Method

- ❖ Grind the mustard seeds with the green chillies.
- ❖ Prepare a marinade of curd, turmeric powder, chilli powder, mustard-chilli paste and salt. Marinate the fish in the marinade for half an hour.
- ❖ Pour mustard oil over the fish.
- ❖ Steam the fish for about 15 minutes, till it is cooked.

DOI MACHH *(Fish in curd gravy)*

Ingredients

- 1 kg Rohu or Katla pieces
- 1 cup curd
- 2 large onions
- 1 tbsp ginger paste
- 2-3 bay leaves
- 4-5 cloves
- 4 cardamoms
- 2" piece of cinnamon
- 1 tsp chilli powder
- 1 tsp turmeric powder
- Salt to taste
- Oil for cooking

Method

- ❖ Clean and wash the fish pieces. Coat them with turmeric powder and salt.
- ❖ Grind the onions into a fine paste. Beat the curd.
- ❖ Heat some oil in a kadai. Fry the fish pieces on medium flame till they are light brown and done. Take care that they do not break. Remove and keep aside.
- ❖ To the oil, add bay leaves and cardamoms, cloves, cinnamon pieces. Fry for a few seconds and add the onion paste. Fry till the moisture has evaporated. Add the ginger paste and fry for a few minutes.

- ❖ In a teaspoon of water, dissolve the chilli powder and turmeric powder.
- ❖ Add this to the kadai and fry for a minute.
- ❖ Add the fried fish pieces and the curd along with 1 cup of hot water. Let it simmer on low heat.
- ❖ Turn thc fish pieces once. When the curd leaves the oil, take the kadai off the fire.
- ❖ Serve hot with steaming rice.

MACCHER JHOL ***(Fish curry with vegetables)***

Ingredients

- 500 gms fish, cut into pieces
- 1 large cauliflower
- 1 small potato
- 1 small onion
- 10-12 pods of green peas
- 1 clove garlic
- ½ tsp turmeric powder
- 1 tsp red chilli powder
- 1 tsp curd
- 1 tsp garam masala powder
- Salt to taste
- Oil for frying

Method

- ❖ Grind the ginger, garlic and onion. Keep aside.
- ❖ Cut the potatoes into cubes, shell the peas and cut the cauliflower into large florets.
- ❖ Clean the fish, coat it with some salt and turmeric powder.
- ❖ Heat oil in a kadai and fry the fish pieces on both sides lightly. Keep aside.
- ❖ In the same kadai, fry the ginger-garlic-onion paste till the oil floats on top. Add turmeric powder, chilli powder and fry for some more time.
- ❖ Add the vegetables and fry for five minutes. Add curd and salt. Cover and cook on low heat till the curd dries up. Then add some water and cook for a few minutes.
- ❖ When the water begins to boil, add the fish and cook till the vegetables are done.
- ❖ Sprinkle garam masala and serve hot.

MACCHER CHOCHORI

(A spicy, dry fish preparation)

Ingredients

- 1 kg fish, cut into pieces
- 250 gms onions
- 250 gms tomatoes
- 1 tsp turmeric powder
- 5 green chillies
- 2 tbsp mustard oil
- Salt to taste

Method

- Clean and wash the fish pieces.
- Chop the onions and tomatoes into fine pieces. Slit the green chillies.
- In a pan, take the fish pieces and mix in the onions, tomatoes, turmeric, salt and green chillies. Add a little mustard oil and keep aside for half an hour.
- Heat oil in a kadai. Pour the entire marination along with the fish pieces in the hot oil. Fry on low flame till the fish is cooked.
- If the fish pieces break, take them out and keep them aside and continue to fry the masala. When the masala is done, put the fish pieces back in it.
- Serve hot with steaming rice.

DIMER DALNA *(Egg curry)*

Ingredients

- 6 eggs
- 2 tomatoes
- 2 potatoes
- 3 onions
- 2 green chillies
- 1" piece of ginger
- ½ tsp red chilli powder
- 1 tsp turmeric powder
- 1 bay leaf
- ½ tsp cumin seeds
- ½ tsp garam masala powder
- Salt to taste
- Oil for cooking

Method

- Boil the eggs and shell them. Grind together the onion, ginger, cumin seeds. Chop the tomatoes finely.
- Peel the potatoes and cut them into cubes.
- Heat a little oil in a kadai and fry the eggs in it for a minute. Keep aside.
- In the same kadai, heat oil and add the bay leaf . Mix the turmeric powder and chilli powder in a teaspoon of water and add this to the oil. Fry till the masala separates from the oil. Now add the onion, ginger and cumin paste. Fry over low heat till the onions are lightly browned.
- Add the potatoes and the tomatoes. Add a cup of water and cook till the potatoes are almost done. Add the fried eggs and salt. Cover and cook on low heat till the potatoes are done. Sprinkle garam masala and garnish with the slit green chillies.
- Serve hot.

Mishti

BHAPA DOI *(Steamed sweet curd)*

Ingredients

- 3 cups curd
- 1 tin of condensed milk
- 1 pinch cardamom powder
- 1 tbsp raisins
- 1 tbsp almonds

Method

- ❖ Tie the curd in a muslin cloth to drain out the water.
- ❖ Add the condensed milk and cardamom powder to the solid curd. Mix well and steam in a double boiler.
- ❖ Garnish with raisins and almonds. Chill and serve.

CHHANAR PAYESH *(Paneer and milk sweet dish)*

Ingredients

- 250 gms paneer
- 3 cups milk
- ½ cup sugar
- 1 tbsp raisins
- 1 tbsp almonds
- ½ tsp cardamom powder

Method

- ❖ Boil the milk till it is reduced to half its quantity.
- ❖ Crumble the paneer into coarse pieces.
- ❖ Make a syrup by boiling the sugar along with 1 cup of water.
- ❖ Mix the paneer and sugar syrup and blend thoroughly. Add the thickened milk to the paneer mixture and boil until a thick and creamy consistency is obtained.
- ❖ Add the cardamom powder, almonds and the raisins.
- ❖ Chill and serve.

LAVANGO LATIKA
(Paneer and coconut stuffed sweet)

Ingredients

- 2 cups maida
- 1 cup coconut, grated
- ½ tsp baking powder
- ½ cup khoya or paneer, grated
- ¼ tsp cardamom powder
- 2 cups sugar
- 2 tbsp ghee
- A few cloves

Method

- Make a syrup by boiling 2 cups of sugar with 1 cup water. Keep aside.
- Sift the maida along with the baking powder. Knead it to form a dough of medium hardness. Make balls out of the dough. Roll the balls into small rectangles.
- Mix the khoya, the grated coconut and cardamom powder to make the filling.
- Place a little filling in the centre of each rectangle and wrap the sides to form a small, square packet. Pierce the packet at the centre, with a clove.
- Heat ghee in a kadai. Deep-fry the packets till they are golden in colour.
- Soak the latikas in the syrup. Decorate with grated coconut and serve.

ROSOGOLLA ***(Spongy, sweet, paneer balls)***

Ingredients

- ½ litre cow's milk
- 5 ml vinegar

For The Syrup

- ½ kg sugar
- 300 ml water
- 2 tbsp milk

Method

- In a pan boil the sugar along with the water to make the syrup. Add the milk and remove the scum.

- ❖ Boil the milk in another pan. Continue to boil for 30 minutes. Gradually add the vinegar and let the milk curdle. Drain the curdled milk through a fine muslin.
- ❖ Wash the paneer by dipping the muslin bundle into cold water.
- ❖ Dip the paneer in hot water. Now add 15 gms of sugar and knead the paneer till it is soft and smooth and does not have any lumps. Divide it into small portions and roll into balls.
- ❖ Flatten them slightly and add to the syrup. Cook for ten minutes until the balls are spongy. (Whenever the syrup turns frothy, add a little water)

SANDESH *(Paneer sweet dish)*

Ingredients

- 1 litre whole milk
- ¼ cup sugar
- 2 tbsp lime juice
- 2 drops of keora essence
- A few raisins
- A few almonds

Method

- ❖ Boil the milk. Cool and refrigerate overnight. Remove cream and strain the milk.
- ❖ Bring the milk to a boil and lower the heat. Add the lime juice. When the milk curdles, remove from heat and keep aside for one hour.
- ❖ Tie the paneer in a thin muslin cloth and hang it for an hour so that the whey drains out.
- ❖ Cook paneer and sugar over a low heat till the moisture dries up. Add the essence towards the end. Let it cool.
- ❖ Grind the mixture in a mixie until it becomes smooth. Divide into small portions.
- ❖ There are several types of moulds available in the market. You can create beautifully designed sandesh by pressing the mixture into these moulds. Or you can simply make flat balls out of the mixture.

Annexures

Annexure-1

CONVERSIONS

Liquid Measures

1 cup = 16 tbsp

1 cup milk = 250 ml

1 cup oil = 212 gms

1 tbsp = 15 ml

1 tbsp = 3 tsp

1 tbsp oil = 12 gms

1 tbsp = 5 ml

Solid Measures

1 bunch coriander leaves = 85 gms

1 cup flour = 125 gms

1 cup rice = 250 gms

1 cup sugar = 250 gms

1 pod garlic = 15 gms

1 tbsp coriander seeds = 10 gms

1 tbsp flour = 8 gms

1 tbsp ghee = 20 gms

1 tsp coriander seeds = 2 gms

1 tsp ginger powder = 2 gms

1 tsp salt = 15 gms

1 tsp sugar = 5 gms

1" ginger = 3 gms

2" cinnamon piece = 12 gms

5 whole red chillies = 20 gms

GLOSSARY OF COOKERY TERMS

Basting: moistening the meat or poultry with juices during roasting.

Batter: a mixture of dry ingredients and liquid that is stirred or beaten and is of pouring consistency.

Binding: adding liquid, eggs or melted fat to a dry mixture to hold it together.

Blanching: removing the outer skin after plunging it in hot water and then in cold water, eg., blanching of almonds or tomatoes.

Blending: combining the ingredients with a spoon to achieve a uniform consistency.

Browning: searing the outer surface of meat at high flame to seal in the juices.

Chilling: cooling without freezing, in the refrigerator.

Coat: to sprinkle food with or dip it into flour, etc., until completely covered.

Deep-frying: frying by immersing it in hot oil.

Dice: to cut into small pieces.

Dough: a mixture of flour, water or milk which is firm enough to knead and form into shapes.

Dropping consistency: the consistency of cake and pudding mixture before cooking; if a spoonful of mixture is lifted from the bowl. It should drop off the spoon in 5 seconds.

Garnishing: decorating with colourful and contrasting food.

Grating: shredding of foods by rubbing against a grater.

Gravy: thick liquid made by adding water to the masala.

Grilling: cooking directly under a flame or heating in an oven.

Julienne: vegetables cut in thin match-like strips.

Par boiling: boiling for a short time to cook food partially.

Pulp: soft, fleshy tissue of fruits or vegetables.

Puree: liquidised pulp.

Sauté: to fry food rapidly in shallow heat, tossing and turning it until evenly browned.

Shred: cut into strips.

Sift: to shake a dry ingredient through a sieve to remove lumps.

Simmering: cooking in liquid which is heated to just below boiling point.

Skewer: metal or wooden pin used to hold meat, poultry or fish in shape, during cooking.

Stewing: to simmer food slowly in a covered pan.

Stirring: mixing with a circular movement of a spoon.

Straining: separating liquids from solids by passing them through a sieve or through a muslin.

Syrup: a thick sweet liquid made by boiling sugar with water or fruit juices.

Whipping: beating the ingredients until thick and frothy.

Yeast: fungus cells used to produce alcoholic fermentation or to cause the dough to rise.

CALORIE CONTENT OF COMMON FOOD ITEMS IN CONVENIENT MEASURES

A. Raw Foods

Item	Measure	Weight g.	Energy cal.
Cereals			
Rice	1 cup (small)	150	520
Wheat flour	"	90	310
Millet Flour	"	90	300
Pulses			
Bengal gram	"	130	485
Other dals	"	135	460
Whole Pulses			
Greengram	"	140	470
Cowpea (lobia)	"	135	440
Rajma	"	120	415
Soyabean	"	130	530
Green leafy vegetables	5 bundles	100	62
Other vegetables		100	105
Nuts and Oilseeds			
Almonds	10 no.	15	85
Cashewnuts	10 no.	15	95
Coconut (fresh)	1 no.	115	510
Coconut (dry)	1/2 no.	45	290
Groundnuts	50 no.	15	85
Sesame seeds	1 tsp.	3	15
Oils/Vanaspati ghee	2 tsp.	10 ml.	100
Spices			
Chilli powder	1 tsp.	7	17
Coriander seeds	1 tsp.	7	20
Cumin seeds	1 tsp.	5	18
Fenugreek (Methi)	1 tsp.	6	20
Mustard seeds	1 tsp.	10	5

Item	Measure	Weight g.	Energy cal.
Garlic	7 cloves	3	4
Onion	1 med.	50	30
Animal foods			
Egg (hen)	one	60	100
Mutton		100	194
Fish (lean)		100	100
Fish (fatty)		100	150

Notes: tsp: teaspoon (5 ml.), **tbsp:** tablespoon (15 ml.), **1 cup (small)** = 150 ml.

B. Cooked Foods

Item	No. of Serving	Weight gms.	Energy cal.
Cereal preparations			
Rice	1 cup	100	110
Idli	"	60	75
Plain dosa	"	40	125
Masala dosa	"	100	200
Phulka	"	35	80
Paratha	"	50	150
Upma	"	130	200
Sevian upma	"	80	130
Bread toasted	2 slices	50	170
Poha (Awal)	1 cup	100	200
Dalia	"	140	165
Khichidi	"	100	210
Puri	1	25	80
Pulse preparations			
Plain dal	1 cup	140	170
Sambar	"	160	81
Chhole/Sundal	"	150	115
Vegetable preparations			
With gravy	1 cup	130	130

Item	No. of Serving	Weight gms.	Energy cal.
Dry	"	100	115
Bagara Baigan	"	170	230
Vegetable kofta	"	145	220
Fried snacks			
Bhaji	1	7	35
Samosa	1	65	210
Kachori	1	45	200
Potato Bonda	1	40	100
Sago vada	1	30	100
Masala vada	1	20	56
Vada	1	20	65
Dahi vada	1	80	170
Vegetable cutlet	1	30	70
Chutneys			
Coconut/ground nuts/til/coriander	1 tbsp	25	64
Tomato	1 tbsp	20	10
Non-Vegetarian preparations			
Boiled egg	1	50	86
Omelette	1	65	155
Fried egg	1	50	155
Mutton curry	1 cup	145	240
Chicken curry	"	125	260
Fish (fried)	2 pieces	85	220
Bakery products			
Biscuits	2	40	220
Cake	1	40	220
Vegetable puff	1	60	170
Pastry	1	50	350
Mathri	2	75	300
Sweets			
Laddoo, burfi, etc.	1	60	250
Halwa (Suji)	1 cup	130	430

Item	No. of Serving	Weight gms.	Energy cal.
Double ka meetha	"	105	280
Custard/puddings	"	110	180
Chikki	2	60	300
Jam/Jelly	1 tsp.	7	20
Sugar	1 tbsp	15 ml.	20
Honey	1 tbsp	15 ml.	60
Jalebi	2 pieces	100 gm.	500
Gulab Jamun	"	50 gm.	400
Jaggery	1 tbsp.	15 gm.	56

C. Salads

Item	No.	Weight gms.	Energy cal.
Beetroot	1	65	30
Cabbage	1	250	70
Carrot	1	40	20
Cucumber	1	90	12
Lettuce	6 bundles	100	20
Onion	1	50	25
Radish	1	60	10
Tomato	1	50	10
Turnip	1	100	30

D. Fruits

Item	No./ Quantity	Weight gms.	Energy cal.
Apple	1	100	65
Banana	1	80	90
Grapes	30	100	70
Guava	1	100	50
Jackfruit	4 pieces	100	90

Item	No./ Quantity	Weight gms.	Energy cal.
Mango	1	250	180
Mosambi/orange	1	100	40
Papaya	1 piece	250	80
Pineapple	1 piece	100	50
Sapota	1	80	80
Custard apple	1	130	130
Watermelon/Muskmelon	1 piece	100	15

E. Beverages

Item	Measure	Qty. ml.	Energy cal.
Coffee	1 cup	150	100
Tea	1 cup	150	60
Carbonated beverages	1 bottle	200	150
Fresh lime juice	1 glass	200	60
Squash	"	200	80
Syrups (sherbat)	"	200	200
Orange juice	"	200	150

F. Milk and Milk Products

Item	Measure	Qty. ml.	Energy cal.
Milk (buffalo)	1 cup	150 ml.	300
Milk (cow)	"	150 ml.	100
Curd (cow)	"	150 ml.	85
Buttermilk (lassi)	"	150 ml.	45
Paneer	"	100 gm.	350
Ghee	2 tsp	10 ml.	100
Butter	3 tsp	15 ml.	100
Khoya (from whole milk)		100 gm.	400
Khoya (butter separated)		100 gm.	200

Item	Measure	Qty. ml.	Energy cal.
Skimmed milk	1 cup	150 ml.	45
Cream	1 tbsp	15 ml.	50
Cheese	1 packet	30 gm.	100
Rabadi	1 cup	150 gm.	525

Annexure-3

Cholesterol Content of Animal Foods

Item	Fat g/100 g.	Saturated fatty acids g/100 g.	Cholesterol mg/100 g.
Butter	80	50	250
Ghee	100	65	300
Milk (cow)	4	2	14
Milk (buffalo)	8	4	16
Milk (skimmed)	0.1	-	2
Milk (condensed)	10	6	40
Cream	13	8	40
Cheese	25	15	100
Egg (whole)	11	4	400
Egg yolk	30	9	1120
Chicken without skin	4	1	60
Chicken with skin	18	6	100
Beef	16	8	70
Mutton	13	7	65
Pork	35	13	90
Organ meats			
Brain	6	2	2000
Heart	5	2	150
Kidney	2	1	370
Liver	9	3	300
Sea foods			
Prawns/shrimps	2	0.3	150
Fish (lean)	1.5	0.4	45
Fish (fatty)	6	2.5	45

Annexure-4

Nutritive Value of Foods

(Amounts given per 100 gms of edible portion)

Food	Water ml	Calories	Protein gm	Fat gm	Carbo hydrate	Fibre gm	Calcium mg	Iron mg	Vit. A i.u.	B1 mg	B2 mg	Niacin mg	Vit. C mg
1	2	3	4	5	6	7	8	9	10	11	12	13	14
Almond	5	657	20	59	12	1.7	230	4.5	—	.3	.6	4.5	—
Amla	81	55	0.5	.10	14	3.4	50	1.2	—	—	—	—	600
Animal fat	1	891	—	99	—	—	—	—	—	—	—	—	—
Apple	84	61	.3	.4	14	1	4	1	20	.02	.04	.2	5
Apricot	90	36	1	—	8	.4	15	1	2000	.03	.05	.5	5
Bajra millet	13	361	11.6	.5	67.5	1.2	42	5	—	.33	.25	2.3	—
Banana	70	116	1	.3	27	.3	7	.5	100	.1	.08	.8	7
Barley	13	336	22.5	1.3	62.6	3.9	26	8	—	.47	.20	5.4	—
Bathua leaves	90	30	3.7	.4	2.9	.8	150	4.2	—	.01	.14	.6	35
Beetroot	87	45	1.8	—	10	.7	15	1	—	.02	.03	3	5
Black pepper	13	347	.12	7	59	4.9	130	10	—	.04	.2	1	—
Brown Khandsari	1	389	.2	—	97	—	30	2	—	0.2	.1	.3	—

Contd.

Nutritive Value of Foods

(Amounts given per 100 gms of edible portion)

Food	Water ml	Calories	Protein gm	Fat gm	Carbo hydrate	Fibre gm	Calcium mg	Iron mg	Vit. A i.u.	B1 mg	B2 mg	Niacin mg	Vit. C mg
1	2	3	4	5	6	7	8	9	10	11	12	13	14
Butter	16	745	.5	82.5	—	—	15	.2	3000	—	—	—	—
Butter oil, pure	8	828	—	92	—	—	—	—	2000	—	—	—	—
Cane juice	81	73	.3	—	18	—	6	2	—	.02	.02	.1	10
Cardamom, dried	20	228	10	2	43	20	113	5	—	—	—	—	—
Carrot	90	33	1	—	7	.8	40	.7	3000	.05	.05	.5	.6
Cashewnut	5	590	20	45	26	1.3	50	5	--	.6	.2	2.1	—
Cauliflower	90	33	3	.2	5	1	30	1	20	.1	.1	.7	—
Cumin seed	12	356	19	15	36	12	1080	31	300	—	—	2.6	—
Cinnamon	12	229	12	7.8	28	35	440	17	—	.1	.4	2.4	—
Clove	23	293	5	9	48	10	740	5	—	.1	.2	2	—
Coconut Kernel	20	375	4	35	11	4	10	2	—	.05	.02	.6	—
Cucumber	96	12	.6	—	2	.5	15	.3	—	.04	.02	.2	10
Custard apple	75	93	1	—	22	1	25	.5	—	.1	.08	.8	30

Contd.

Nutritive Value of Foods
(Amounts given per 100 gms of edible portion)

Food	Water ml	Calories	Protein gm	Fat gm	Carbo hydrate	Fibre gm	Calcium mg	Iron mg	Vit. A i.u.	B1 mg	B2 mg	Niacin mg	Vit. C mg
1	2	3	4	5	6	7	8	9	10	11	12	13	14
Dried dates	20	303	2	—	74	2.4	70	2	50	.07	.05	2	—
Dried pea	10	337	25	1	57	4.5	70	5	100	.8	.2	2.5	—
Eggplant (brinjal)	93	22	1	—	4	1	10	1	—	.05	.03	.8	5
Fig, dried	20	269	4	—	63	11	200	4	100	.1	.08	1.7	—
Fig, fresh	85	49	1.3	—	11	2	50	1	80	.05	.05	.4	2
Fresh beans & peas	70	104	7	—	19	2.5	40	15	500	.3	.15	1.5	25
Fresh mushroom	91	13	2.5	.3	—	1	20	1	—	.12	.5	5.8	3
Garlic	63	139	6	—	29	.8	13	1.3	—	.25	.08	.4	10
Gourd	92	28	.7	—	6	.3	20	.6	—	.04	.03	.6	15
Gram, whole	10	338	22	.5	61	5.3	280	8	40	.4	.15	2.5	—
Moong bean (Green)	12	324	22	1	57	4.7	100	8	40	.45	.2	2	—
Grape	80	76	1	—	18	.5	20	.3	50	.04	.02	.3	5
Green pepper	90	37	2	.5	6	1	20	1	130-800	.03	.03	.3	150
Green spring onion	90	36	1.8	.5	6	1	40	3	500	.05	.1	.5	50

Contd.

Nutritive Value of Foods
(Amounts given per 100 gms of edible portion)

Food	Water ml	Calories	Protein gm	Fat gm	Carbo hydrate	Fibre gm	Calcium mg	iron mg	Vit. A i.u.	B1 mg	B2 mg	Niacin mg	Vit. C mg
1	2	3	4	5	6	7	8	9	10	11	12	13	14
Groundnut	6	579	27	45	17	3	50	2.5	—	.9	.15	17	—
Guava	80	58	1	.4	13	5.5	15	1	200	.05	.04	1	200
Honey	23	286	4	—	76	—	5	.4	—	—	.05	.2	—
Jam	29	260	.4	—	69	.6	12	.3	—	—	—	—	10
Lemon	85	55	1.1	0.9	11.1	1.7	70	2.3	—	—	—	—	39
Lettuce	94	19	1.4	—	3	.5	35	2.4	300	.1	.1	.4	15
Lichi	82	71	.9	.5	16	.3	5	.5	—	.04	.04	.3	50
Lobia bean	12	323	24.1	1	54.5	3.8	77	5.9	60	.51	.2	1.3	—
(black kidney bean)	11	329	24	1	56	4.5	150	9	40	.4	.2	2	—
Maize, whole	12	363	10	4.5	71	2	12	2.5	—	.35	.13	2	—
Mango	83	63	.5	—	15	.8	10	.5	600	.03	.04	.3	30
Mustard leaves	85	34	4	.6	3.2	.8	155	16.3	—	.03	—	—	33
Melon seeds (without skin)	6	581	25	45	19	2	50	8	—	.2	.15	1.5	—

Contd.

Nutritive Value of Foods

(Amounts given per 100 gms of edible portion)

Food	Water ml	Calories	Protein gm	Fat gm	Carbo hydrate	Fibre gm	Calcium mg	Iron mg	Vit. A i.u.	B1 mg	B2 mg	Niacin mg	Vit. C mg
1	2	3	4	5	6	7	8	9	10	11	12	13	14
Methi leaves	85	49	4.4	.9	6	1.1	395	16.5	—	.04	.31	.8	52
Musk-melon	93	26	.5	—	6	.4	10	.4	500	.03	.03	.5	30
Orange, Malta	86	53	.8	—	13	.3	30	.5	30	.08	.03	.2	45
Papaya	89	39	.8	—	9	.7	20	.5	1000	.03	.03	.2	50
Peach	85	56	.8	—	13	.5	8	.5	300	.02	.03	.3	10
Pear	84	59	.3	—	15	.9	7	.4	—	.02	.02	.2	4
Pineapple	85	57	.4	—	14	.5	20	.5	100	.08	.03	.1	30
Pistachio	6	626	20	54	15	2	140	14	100	7	.5	1.5	—
Plum	88	45	.7	—	11	.4	10	.4	30	.02	.03	.3	5
Pomegranate	80	77	1	—	18	.2	3	.7	—	.02	.02	.2	8
Potato	80	75	2	—	17	.4	10	.7	—	.1	.03	1.5	15
Pumpkin seeds (without skin)	4	610	30	50	10	2	40	10	30	.2	.2	2	—
Radish	94	18	1	—	4	.7	30	1	—	.03	.03	.3	25
Red kidney bean	12	346	22.9	1.3	60.6	4.5	260	5.8	60	—	—	—	—

Contd.

Nutritive Value of Foods

(Amounts given per 100 gms of edible portion)

Food	Water ml	Calories	Protein gm	Fat gm	Carbo hydrate	Fibre gm	Calcium mg	Iron mg	Vit. A i.u.	B1 mg	B2 mg	Niacin mg	Vit. C mg
1	2	3	4	5	6	7	8	9	10	11	12	13	14
Rice, lightly milled	12	354	8	1.5	77	.5	10	2	—	.25	.05	2	—
Sorghum, Jowar	12	353	10	2.5	73	1.5	20	4	—	.4	.1	3	—
Soyabean	8	382	35	18	20	4.5	200	7-11	—	1.1	.3	2	—
Spinach	85	48	5	.7	5	1.5	250	10.9	3000	.1	.3	1.5	100
Sugar white	—	400	—	—	100	—	—	—	—	—	—	—	—
Sweet Lemon (Mosambi)	84.6	55	1.5	1.0	10.9	1.3	90	.3	26	.04	—	.2	63
Sweet potato	70	114	1.5	.3	26	1	25	1	100	.1	.04	.7	30
Tamarind	20	304	2	—	74	2	50	3	50	.4	.15	1.5	10
Tomato	94	20	1	—	4	.6	5	.4	250	.06	.04	.7	25
Turnip	90	34	1	—	8	.7	30	.4	—	.06	.04	.7	25
Walnut	3	697	15	65	13	2.1	80	2	—	.4	.1	.7	—
Wheat flour, whole	13	341	10	1	75	—	16	1.5	—	.08	.05	.8	—
Wheat, sprouted	13	397	29.2	7.4	53.3	1.4	40	6	—	1.4	.54	2.9	—
Wheat, whole	13	344	11.5	2	70	2	30	3.5	—	.4	.1	5	—
Yam	73	104	2	.2	24	.5	10	1.2	20	.1	.03	.4	10